COSORI Air Fryer Toaster Oven Cookbook 2020

Quick, Easy and Healthy Recipes to Air Fry, Bake, Broil, and Roast with Your COSORI Oven

By Katerina Thompson

Copyrights©2020 By Katerina Thompson

All Rights Reserved

This document is geared towards providing exact and reliable information in regards to the topic and issue covered. The publication is sold with the idea that the publisher is not required to render accounting, officially permitted, or otherwise, qualified services. If advice is necessary, legal or professional, a practiced individual in the profession should be ordered.

Legal Notice: The book is copyright protected. This is only for personal use. You cannot amend, distribute, sell, use, quote or paraphrase any part of the content within this book without the consent of the author.

Under no circumstance will any legal responsibility or blame be held against the publisher for any reparation, damages, or monetary loss due to the information herein, either directly or indirectly.

Disclaimer Notice: Please note the information contained within this document is for educational and entertainment purpose only. Every attempt has been made to provide accurate, up to date and reliable complete information. No warranties of any kind are expressed or implied. Reader acknowledge that the author is not engaging in the rendering of legal, financial, medical or professional advice. The content of this book has been derived from various sources. Please consult a licensed professional before attempting any techniques outlined in this book.

CONTENT

1	*Introduction*
3	**Chapter 1** COSORI Air Fryer 101
10	**Chapter 2** Fast and Easy Everyday Favorites
17	**Chapter 3** Appetizers and Snacks
25	**Chapter 4** Breakfasts
32	**Chapter 5** Vegetables and Sides
39	**Chapter 6** Wraps and Sandwiches
47	**Chapter 7** Poultry
55	**Chapter 8** Meats
65	**Chapter 9** Fish and Seafood
76	**Chapter 10** Rotisserie Recipes
86	**Chapter 11** Desserts
94	**Chapter 12** Holiday Specials
102	**Chapter 13** Sauces, Dips, and Dressings
107	*Appendix 1 Measurement Conversion Chart*
108	*Appendix 2 Air Fryer Cooking Chart*
110	*Appendix 3 Recipe Index*

Introduction

Do you know that the new COSORI Air Fryer Toaster Oven has 12 unique functions?

Are you looking for a simple and basic guide on what all you can do with your COSORI?

Well, if the answer to both the questions above is yes, then you are in the right place. This cookbook will offer you insights into the different functions of COSORI along with suggesting the best recipes that you can make with it.

This cookbook has everything that you need to know about COSORI. Starting from the basic introduction to how to use, benefits, safety features, precautions, and a

This book is a detailed account of my experience with this fantastic device. I am very excited to share the details and usage pattern of my new COSORI with you. Not only this, but I have also added a number of recipes that you can prepare with this device. Also, all these recipes are separated further into subcategories for your help.

Here's everything that you can expect to see in the book:

- Usage guide about the COSORI Air Fryer Toaster Oven
- Specifications and Dimensions of the device
- Benefits of having the COSORI Air Fryer in your kitchen
- A brief about all the functions that you can use with this device
- List of 120 recipes that you can prepare with this device

This is a cookbook that has a lot to offer. And if you have a COSORI Air Fryer Toaster Oven, then this cookbook is the next best thing that you need to buy along with it. Order your today!!

Chapter 1 COSORI Air Fryer 101

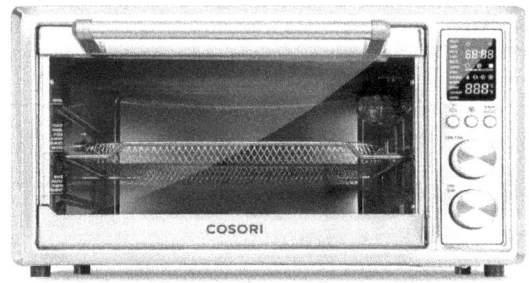

What is COSORI Air Fryer Toaster Oven?

Isn't it amazing that you are getting an Air Fryer, an oven and a toaster in one device? Well, COSORI has brought a fantastic appliance that can cover up to 12 functions required by every cook. To name them all, Toast, Bagel, Pizza, Bake, Roast, Air Fry, Broil, Cookies, Rotisserie, Dehydrate, Ferment, and lastly, Keep Warm. All these 12 presets are embedded into one appliance so that is easier for everyone to prepare their favorite dishes without meddling with different tools and devices only to get confused. So, why not bring home one device that can cover it all for you. Let's know everything you need to know about your new device.

Well, to answer it in a few words, this device is the panacea for all normal and everyday kitchen functions. Along with 12 preset modes, you are also getting a larger capacity oven and toaster. To help you better understand, you can put an entire chicken inside it. Other than this, your new air fryer toaster oven can also accommodate a 33 cm pizza or even 6 pieces of toast inside. So, now it is super easy to host a family dinner without worrying about how you will manage it all.

Further, you can arrange up to three racks in the oven which makes the device versatile enough to combine three appliances into one. And yes, this COSORI Air Fryer Oven Toaster is better than others because of its fast heating and convectional heat circulation system.

The 360° heating and dual fan speed allow you to cook food that is crispier and has a better texture and form. Moreover, with air frying your food will have 85% less fat than what you will get in other forms of frying. So, if you want to maintain your health and do not want the cholesterol levels to spike up further posing a threat to your heart, it is better to switch to air frying today.

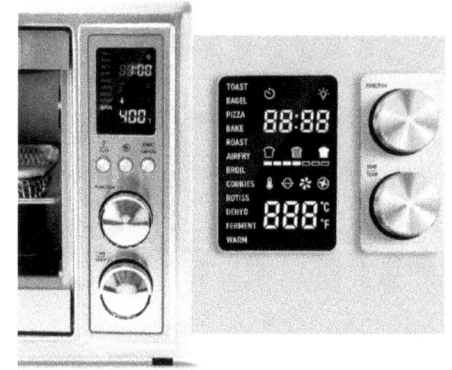

COSORI has added a lot of new features and functionalities to this device. For instance, you will get an LED display, easier controls, there are various accessories, cleaning tools, and much more. This device is designed to become an efficient kitchen and take care of every small or big task that needs to be done.

Usage and Benefits

Ok, where shall I start? Because there is a lot to talk about. Well, beginning from the basic functions in the COSORI Air Fryer Toaster Oven:

- **Toast:** The Toaster can be used to either make some crispy bread toasts or even to prepare bread. You can use the toaster for bread browning and defrost foods. Other than this, using the toast function can also preheat the oven for some baking adventures.

- **Bagel:** Well, as the name suggests with Bagel function you can toast the bagels, especially from the inside. Other than this, you can also use the Bagel function to toast bread.

- **Pizza:** Homemade pizza can be an exciting and amazing experience with this toaster oven. With this mode, you will get perfectly melted cheese and finely crisped pizza crust.

- **Bake:** Who doesn't like cake? Well, you can use the bake function for only preparing a cake, but also for cooking foods, muffins, and pastries.

- **Roast:** Meats and Poultry lovers, here comes yet another fantastic device from COSORI that will quench your thirst for a perfectly roasted meat. The meat roasted in this appliance is juicier, tender and has a perfect blend of taste and crispiness overall.

- **Air Fry:** The Air Fryer is new and not to mention an excellent addition to the appliance. Also, you will get an automatic preheat function with the Air Fryer system. Use this for preparing dishes that have less fat, are crispier, better, and lip-smackingly tastier.

- **Broil:** For browning the upper layers of desserts and casseroles you can use the Broil function. Moreover, it can also be used for preparing sandwiches, meat, fish, bacon, and other such items.

- **Cookies:** If you are looking for perfection, then use the Cookies function to prepare the best cookies in your neighborhood. Now, you won't need an occasion to prepare cookies. You can make them anytime and that too super comfortably. Also, the Cookies function also has an automatic preheat function embedded in the system.

- **Rotisserie:** Rotisserie is the best function for a dish that needs to be roasted from all sides, more like a rotating roast.

- **Dehydrate:** With frozen foods, dehydrating is always essential if you want to eat an evenly cooked and well-prepared dish. You can use this function to bring the ingredients to normal without cooking them.

- **Ferment:** You must know that fermenting the yeast for making bread or pizza dough takes a lot of time. But when you keep it inside this toaster oven, it can be done within as less as 30 minutes. It can also depend on the quantity and the type of dish that you want to prepare with it.

- **Warm:** This is more like keep warm. With this function, you can make sure that the food you have prepared earlier stays warm for longer hours without overcooking. Just select the Keep Warm function, choose the temperature and the appliance will take care of the rest.

So, after going through these 12 presets, there are a lot of benefits accorded to this appliance:

- **Fan Speed:** With the Dehydrate and Air Frying functions the fan speed is set automatically. The most important benefit of this fan speed is that the food will get heat evenly on all the nooks and corners.

- **Automatic Preheat:** There are in total 6 presets that have automatic preheat. This provides the user with an additional support system for better cooking. Here you have to take note that if you would press the Start or Stop button while it is preheating, then it will stop immediately.

- **Multifunctionality:** Another important aspect is that this Air Fryer Oven can perform different functions. Moreover, all these functions have dedicated tools and trays to cook your food. You have the crumb tray, air fryer basket, food tray, wire rack, and Rotisserie Fork Set and handles.

- People also love the fact that you can see the food being prepared inside the oven toaster.

- Lastly, the rotisserie and the dehydrator functions are some of the best additions to the oven toaster. And I personally also love to use these functions in my COSORI Air Fryer Toaster Oven.

How does it work?

This section will explain the functioning and mechanism of the new COSORI Air Fryer Toaster Oven. There are three different slots for different kinds of trays that can be fitted into the oven.

The working mechanism of the toaster, oven, and the air fryer is similar to each other. In this device, the heat is generated through the element and a fan distributes it evenly throughout the appliance. And this is the case with every function. Be it roasting or broiling or anything else.

Once you have put the dish on any kind of tray and set the function, the device will start and set the temperature itself. Even though it is set automatically, you can change it if you want to.

Moreover, when you start the device and set the function it will work accordingly. For some functions preheating is essential and the COSORI will take care of it. There are two knobs in the device that will help you set the temperature and timer.

The LED display will further help you analyze how much time is left, what function is the appliance working on. So in a sense, everything is there in front of you to check.

This device is very simple and straightforward to operate. All you need to do is understand its 12 functions and know how to use them effectively. I am writing this book to help people like you and me who are new to working with a multifunctional appliance. There are a lot of aspects when you are operating such a device and that is why my aim is to give you an overview of all its functions and what all you can do with this device.

Features and Specifications

Let's go through some amazing features of the COSORI Air Fryer Toaster Oven:

- Starting with the elegant design and higher performance, the COSORI Air Fryer Toaster Oven is bigger and better than its counterparts. The stainless steel body and non-stick interiors, and a rugged glass door further make it look a lot better in the kitchen.

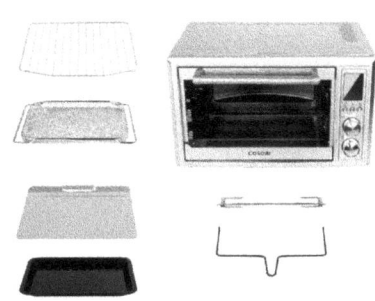

- The size of this appliance allows an everyday user to work smoothly in a kitchen. Yes, the size is a bit bigger than a normal oven, but you are saving the space of three different appliances by using one.

- There are different sized baskets, trays, and utensils that come along with the purchase. Every basket has a different function and holds a different kind of food. So, it is essential that you understand the role of each of these trays before using it.

- On the bottom, there is a removable crumb tray. This is a great addition found in very few ovens and toasters. The removable crumb tray will prevent drips of your favorite turkey from dropping on the oven bottom making it difficult to clean.

Safety Features and Precautions

A device that has multiple functions and operations needs to operate safely and securely. Added to this, you also need to work carefully with it. So, here are some safety precautions that you need to know about:

- Make sure that you unplug the device before you start to clean it. This is to prevent any kind of electrocution incident.

- Also, if you need to take out all the extra trays and parts for cleaning purposes, make sure to let it cool down first and then go ahead with it.

- Always ensure that the power cords, oven parts, and other such electrical terminals are not immersed in water.

- One of the most important safety features is not to use any kind of third party parts for the air fryer toaster oven.

- This appliance is best to use indoors and you should not take it outside for cooking.

- The upper surface of the device is always hot when it is in use. So, best not keep anything on the top of the oven when you are using it. Further, keep the kids away from it as the mirror glass can also get very hot when it is in use.

- It is essential that you clean the crumb tray every time after using the device. The thing is that these crumbs may heat up excessively and they are susceptible to catch fire.

So, now you must have gotten a brief idea about the versatility, operational capacity, and safety functions of this device. There is no doubt that you will be working with one of the best air fryer toaster ovens in the market. This oven has a lot of features and functions that you can work with.

After reading the basic information about the device, you will also find around 80 recipes that are separated breakfast, appetizers, snacks, beef, lamb, pork, desserts, vegan food, and fish & seafood.

FAQs

What are the Dimensions of the COSORI Air Fryer Toaster Oven?

Well, this appliance is measured 22.3 x 19.3 x 16.3 inches. In terms of the volume, capacity is 30 L and further, the weight is 25.4 pounds. Yes, it is big but you can also have the benefits and functions of three different appliances in one.

Can I use a Parchment Paper while cooking in the oven?

Yes, you can use it. But make sure that you do not place the parchment paper inside the oven without putting on top of it. The reason being that it can get heated up and blown all around the oven due to air that runs inside.

CHAPTER 2

FAST AND EASY EVERYDAY FAVORITES

12	Sweet Corn and Carrot Fritters
12	Air Fried Broccoli
13	Bistro Potato Wedges
13	Cheesy Sausage Balls
14	Carrot and Celery Croquettes
14	Bacon-Wrapped Beef Hot Dog
15	Cheesy Potato Patties
15	Simple Pea Delight
16	Easy Roasted Asparagus
16	Baked Chorizo Scotch Eggs

Sweet Corn and Carrot Fritters

Prep time: 10 minutes | Cook time: 10 minutes | Serves 4

- 1 medium-sized carrot, grated
- 1 yellow onion, finely chopped
- 4 ounces (113 g) canned sweet corn kernels, drained
- 1 teaspoon sea salt flakes
- 1 tablespoon chopped fresh cilantro
- 1 medium-sized egg, whisked
- 2 tablespoons plain milk
- 1 cup grated Parmesan cheese
- ¼ cup flour
- ⅓ teaspoon baking powder
- ⅓ teaspoon sugar
- Cooking spray

1. Press Start/Cancel. Preheat the air fryer oven to 350ºF (177ºC).
2. Place the grated carrot in a colander and press down to squeeze out any excess moisture. Dry it with a paper towel.
3. Combine the carrots with the remaining ingredients.
4. Mold 1 tablespoon of the mixture into a ball and press it down with your hand or a spoon to flatten it. Repeat until the rest of the mixture is used up.
5. Spritz the balls with cooking spray.
6. Arrange in the fry basket, taking care not to overlap any balls. Insert at low position.
7. Select Bake, Convection, and set time to 10 minutes, or until they're firm.
8. Serve warm.

Air Fried Broccoli

Prep time: 5 minutes | Cook time: 6 minutes | Serves 1

- 4 egg yolks
- ¼ cup butter, melted
- 2 cups coconut flower
- Salt and pepper, to taste
- 2 cups broccoli florets

1. Press Start/Cancel. Preheat the air fryer oven to 400ºF (204ºC).
2. In a bowl, whisk the egg yolks and melted butter together. Throw in the coconut flour, salt and pepper, then stir again to combine well.
3. Dip each broccoli floret into the mixture and place in the fry basket. Insert the fry basket at mid position. Select Air Fry, Convection, and set time to 6 minutes. work in batches if necessary. Take care when removing them from the air fryer oven and serve immediately.

Bistro Potato Wedges

Prep time: 10 minutes | Cook time: 13 minutes | Serves 4

- 1 pound (454 g) fingerling potatoes, cut into wedges
- 1 teaspoon extra-virgin olive oil
- ½ teaspoon garlic powder
- Salt and pepper, to taste
- ½ cup raw cashews, soaked in water overnight
- ½ teaspoon ground turmeric
- ½ teaspoon paprika
- 1 tablespoon nutritional yeast
- 1 teaspoon fresh lemon juice
- 2 tablespoons to ¼ cup water

1. Press Start/Cancel. Preheat the air fryer oven to 400ºF (204ºC).
2. In a bowl, toss together the potato wedges, olive oil, garlic powder, and salt and pepper, making sure to coat the potatoes well.
3. Transfer the potatoes to the fry basket and insert the fry basket at mid position. Select Air Fry, Convection, and set time to 10 minutes.
4. In the meantime, prepare the cheese sauce. Pulse the cashews, turmeric, paprika, nutritional yeast, lemon juice, and water together in a food processor. Add more water to achieve your desired consistency.
5. When the potatoes are finished cooking, transfer to a bowl and add the cheese sauce on top. Air fry for an additional 3 minutes.
6. Serve hot.

Cheesy Sausage Balls

Prep time: 5 minutes | Cook time: 15 minutes | Serves 6

- 12 ounces (340 g) Jimmy Dean's Sausage
- 6 ounces (170 g) shredded Cheddar cheese
- 10 Cheddar cubes

1. Press Start/Cancel. Preheat the air fryer oven to 375ºF (191ºC).
2. Mix the shredded cheese and sausage.
3. Divide the mixture into 12 equal parts to be stuffed.
4. Add a cube of cheese to the center of the sausage and roll into balls. Transfer the balls to the fry basket.
5. Insert the fry basket at mid position. Select Air Fry, Convection, and set time to 15 minutes, or until crisp.
6. Serve immediately.

Carrot and Celery Croquettes

Prep time: 10 minutes | Cook time: 6 minutes | Serves 4

- 2 medium-sized carrots, trimmed and grated
- 2 medium-sized celery stalks, trimmed and grated
- ½ cup finely chopped leek
- 1 tablespoon garlic paste
- ¼ teaspoon freshly cracked black pepper
- 1 teaspoon fine sea salt
- 1 tablespoon finely chopped fresh dill
- 1 egg, lightly whisked
- ¼ cup flour
- ¼ teaspoon baking powder
- ½ cup bread crumbs
- Cooking spray
- Chive mayo, for serving

1. Press Start/Cancel. Preheat the air fryer oven to 360ºF (182ºC).
2. Drain any excess liquid from the carrots and celery by placing them on a paper towel.
3. Stir together the vegetables with all of the other ingredients, save for the bread crumbs and chive mayo.
4. Use your hands to mold 1 tablespoon of the vegetable mixture into a ball and repeat until all of the mixture has been used up. Press down on each ball with your hand or a palette knife. Cover completely with bread crumbs. Spritz the croquettes with cooking spray.
5. Arrange the croquettes in a single layer in the fry basket and insert the fry basket at mid position. Select Air Fry, Convection, and set time to 6 minutes.
6. Serve warm with the chive mayo on the side.

Bacon-Wrapped Beef Hot Dog

Prep time: 5 minutes | Cook time: 10 minutes | Serves 4

- 4 slices sugar-free bacon
- 4 beef hot dogs

1. Press Start/Cancel. Preheat the air fryer oven to 370ºF (188ºC).
2. Take a slice of bacon and wrap it around the hot dog, securing it with a toothpick. Repeat with the other pieces of bacon and hot dogs, placing each wrapped dog in the fry basket. Insert at low position.
3. Select Bake, Convection, and set time to 10 minutes, turning halfway through.
4. Once hot and crispy, the hot dogs are ready to serve.

Cheesy Potato Patties

Prep time: 5 minutes | Cook time: 10 minutes | Serves 8

- 2 pounds (907 g) white potatoes
- ½ cup finely chopped scallions
- ½ teaspoon freshly ground black pepper, or more to taste
- 1 tablespoon fine sea salt
- ½ teaspoon hot paprika
- 2 cups shredded Colby cheese
- ¼ cup canola oil
- 1 cup crushed crackers

1. Press Start/Cancel. Preheat the air fryer oven to 360ºF (182ºC).
2. Boil the potatoes until soft. Dry them off and peel them before mashing thoroughly, leaving no lumps.
3. Combine the mashed potatoes with scallions, pepper, salt, paprika, and cheese.
4. Mold the mixture into balls with your hands and press with your palm to flatten them into patties.
5. In a shallow dish, combine the canola oil and crushed crackers. Coat the patties in the crumb mixture. Transfer the patties to the food tray. Insert the food tray at low position.
6. Select Bake, Convection, and set time to 10 minutes. You may need to work in batches.
7. Serve hot.

Simple Pea Delight

Prep time: 5 minutes | Cook time: 15 minutes | Serves 2 to 4

- 1 cup flour
- 1 teaspoon baking powder
- 3 eggs
- 1 cup coconut milk
- 1 cup cream cheese
- 3 tablespoons pea protein
- ½ cup chicken or turkey strips
- Pinch of sea salt
- 1 cup Mozzarella cheese

1. Press Start/Cancel. Preheat the air fryer oven to 390ºF (199ºC).
2. In a large bowl, mix all ingredients together using a large wooden spoon.
3. Spoon equal amounts of the mixture into muffin cups and place the cups in the food tray. Insert at low position.
4. Select Bake, Convection, and set time to 15 minutes.
5. Serve immediately.

Easy Roasted Asparagus

Prep time: 5 minutes | Cook time: 7 minutes | Serves 4

- 1 pound (454 g) asparagus, trimmed and halved crosswise
- 1 teaspoon extra-virgin olive oil
- Salt and pepper, to taste
- Lemon wedges, for serving

1. Press Start/Cancel. Preheat the air fryer oven to 400ºF (204ºC).
2. Toss the asparagus with the oil, ⅛ teaspoon salt, and ⅛ teaspoon pepper in bowl. Transfer to fry basket.
3. Place the basket in air fryer oven and insert at low position. Select Roast, Convection, and set time to 7 minutes, or until tender and bright green, tossing halfway through cooking.
4. Season with salt and pepper and serve with lemon wedges.

Baked Chorizo Scotch Eggs

Prep time: 5 minutes | Cook time: 18 minutes | Makes 4 eggs

- 1 pound (454 g) Mexican chorizo or other seasoned sausage meat
- 4 soft-boiled eggs plus 1 raw egg
- 1 tablespoon water
- ½ cup all-purpose flour
- 1 cup panko bread crumbs
- Cooking spray

1. Divide the chorizo into 4 equal portions. Flatten each portion into a disc. Place a soft-boiled egg in the center of each disc. Wrap the chorizo around the egg, encasing it completely. Place the encased eggs on a plate and chill for at least 30 minutes.
2. Press Start/Cancel. Preheat the air fryer oven to 360ºF (182ºC).
3. Beat the raw egg with 1 tablespoon of water. Place the flour on a small plate and the panko on a second plate. Working with 1 egg at a time, roll the encased egg in the flour, then dip it in the egg mixture. Dredge the egg in the panko and place on a plate. Repeat with the remaining eggs.
4. Spray the eggs with oil and place in the fry basket. Insert at low position. Select Bake, Convection, and set time to 10 minutes. Turn and bake for an additional 8 minutes, or until browned and crisp on all sides.
5. Serve immediately.

CHAPTER 3

APPETIZERS AND SNACKS

19 Spiced Mixed Nuts
19 Crispy Spiced Chickpeas
20 Spicy Chicken Wings
20 Coconut-Crusted Shrimp
21 Spiced Sweet Potato Fries
22 Rosemary-Garlic Shoestring Fries
22 Baked Ricotta
23 Lemony Chicken Drumsticks
23 Beef and Mango Skewers
24 Shishito Peppers with Herb Dressing

Spiced Mixed Nuts

Prep time: 5 minutes | Cook time: 6 minutes | Makes 2 cups

- ½ cup raw cashews
- ½ cup raw pecan halves
- ½ cup raw walnut halves
- ½ cup raw whole almonds
- 2 tablespoons olive oil
- 1 tablespoon light brown sugar
- 1 teaspoon chopped fresh rosemary leaves
- 1 teaspoon chopped fresh thyme leaves
- 1 teaspoon kosher salt
- ½ teaspoon ground coriander
- ¼ teaspoon onion powder
- ¼ teaspoon freshly ground black pepper
- ⅛ teaspoon garlic powder

1. Press Start/Cancel. Preheat the air fryer oven to 350ºF (177ºC).
2. In a large bowl, combine all the ingredients and toss until the nuts are evenly coated in the herbs, spices, and sugar.
3. Scrape the nuts and seasonings into the fry basket and insert the fry basket at mid position. Select Air Fry, Convection, and set time to 6 minutes, or until golden brown and fragrant, shaking the basket halfway through.
4. Transfer the cocktail nuts to a bowl and serve warm.

Crispy Spiced Chickpeas

Prep time: 5 minutes | Cook time: 9 minutes | Makes 1½ cups

- 1 can (15-ounce / 425-g) chickpeas, rinsed and dried with paper towels
- 1 tablespoon olive oil
- ½ teaspoon dried rosemary
- ½ teaspoon dried parsley
- ½ teaspoon dried chives
- ¼ teaspoon mustard powder
- ¼ teaspoon sweet paprika
- ¼ teaspoon cayenne pepper
- Kosher salt and freshly ground black pepper, to taste

1. Press Start/Cancel. Preheat the air fryer oven to 350ºF (177ºC).
2. In a large bowl, combine all the ingredients, except for the kosher salt and black pepper, and toss until the chickpeas are evenly coated in the herbs and spices.
3. Scrape the chickpeas and seasonings into the fry basket and insert the fry basket at mid position. Select Air Fry, Convection, and set time to 9 minutes, or until browned and crisp, shaking the basket halfway through.
4. Transfer the crispy chickpeas to a bowl, sprinkle with kosher salt and black pepper, and serve warm.

Spicy Chicken Wings

Prep time: 5 minutes | Cook time: 20 minutes | Serves 2 to 4

- 1¼ pounds (567 g) chicken wings, separated into flats and drumettes
- 1 teaspoon baking powder
- 1 teaspoon cayenne pepper
- ¼ teaspoon garlic powder
- Kosher salt and freshly ground black pepper, to taste
- 1 tablespoon unsalted butter, melted

For serving:
- Blue cheese dressing
- Celery
- Carrot sticks

1. Place the chicken wings on a large plate, then sprinkle evenly with the baking powder, cayenne, and garlic powder. Toss the wings with your hands, making sure the baking powder and seasonings fully coat them, until evenly incorporated. Let the wings stand in the refrigerator for 1 hour or up to overnight.
2. Press Start/Cancel. Preheat the air fryer oven to 400ºF (204ºC).
3. Season the wings with salt and black pepper, then transfer to the air fryer oven, standing them up on end against the fry basket wall and each other. Insert the fry basket at mid position.
4. Select Air Fry, Convection, and set time to 20 minutes, or until the wings are cooked through and crisp and golden brown. Transfer the wings to a bowl and toss with the butter while they're hot.
5. Arrange the wings on a platter and serve warm with the blue cheese dressing, celery and carrot sticks.

Coconut-Crusted Shrimp

Prep time: 10 minutes | Cook time: 4 minutes | Serves 2 to 4

- ½ pound (227 g) medium shrimp, peeled and deveined (tails intact)
- 1 cup canned coconut milk
- Finely grated zest of 1 lime
- Kosher salt, to taste
- ½ cup panko bread crumbs
- ½ cup unsweetened shredded coconut
- Freshly ground black pepper, to taste
- Cooking spray
- 1 small or ½ medium cucumber, halved and deseeded
- 1 cup coconut yogurt
- 1 serrano chile, deseeded and minced

1. Press Start/Cancel. Preheat the air fryer oven to 400ºF (204ºC).
2. In a bowl, combine the shrimp, coconut milk, lime zest, and ½ teaspoon kosher salt. Let the shrimp stand for 10 minutes.
3. Meanwhile, in a separate bowl, stir together the bread crumbs and shredded coconut and season with salt and pepper.
4. A few at a time, add the shrimp to the bread crumb mixture and toss to coat completely. Transfer the shrimp to a wire rack set over a baking sheet. Spray the shrimp all over with cooking spray.
5. Transfer the shrimp to the fry basket and insert the fry basket at mid position. Select Air Fry, Convection, and set time to 4 minutes, or until golden brown and cooked through. Transfer the shrimp to a serving platter and season with more salt.
6. Grate the cucumber into a small bowl. Stir in the coconut yogurt and chile and season with salt and pepper. Serve alongside the shrimp while they're warm.

Spiced Sweet Potato Fries

Prep time: 10 minutes | Cook time: 15 minutes | Serves 2

- 2 tablespoons olive oil
- 1½ teaspoons smoked paprika
- 1½ teaspoons kosher salt, plus more as needed
- 1 teaspoon chili powder
- ½ teaspoon ground cumin
- ½ teaspoon ground turmeric
- ½ teaspoon mustard powder
- ¼ teaspoon cayenne pepper
- 2 medium sweet potatoes (about 10 ounces / 284 g each), cut into wedges, ½ inch thick and 3 inches long
- Freshly ground black pepper, to taste
- ⅔ cup sour cream
- 1 garlic clove, grated

1. Press Start/Cancel. Preheat the air fryer oven to 400ºF (204ºC).
2. In a large bowl, combine the olive oil, paprika, salt, chili powder, cumin, turmeric, mustard powder, and cayenne. Add the sweet potatoes, season with black pepper, and toss to evenly coat.
3. Transfer the sweet potatoes to the fry basket (save the bowl with the leftover oil and spices) and insert the fry basket at mid position.
4. Select Air Fry, Convection, and set time to 15 minutes, shaking the basket halfway through, or until golden brown and crisp. Return the potato wedges to the reserved bowl and toss again while they are hot.
5. Meanwhile, in a small bowl, stir together the sour cream and garlic. Season with salt and black pepper and transfer to a serving dish.
6. Serve the potato wedges hot with the garlic sour cream.

Rosemary-Garlic Shoestring Fries

Prep time: 5 minutes | Cook time: 18 minutes | Serves 2

- 1 large russet potato (about 12 ounces / 340 g), scrubbed clean, and julienned
- 1 tablespoon vegetable oil
- Leaves from 1 sprig fresh rosemary
- Kosher salt and freshly ground black pepper, to taste
- 1 garlic clove, thinly sliced
- Flaky sea salt, for serving

1. Press Start/Cancel. Preheat the air fryer oven to 400ºF (204ºC).
2. Place the julienned potatoes in a large colander and rinse under cold running water until the water runs clear. Spread the potatoes out on a double-thick layer of paper towels and pat dry.
3. In a large bowl, combine the potatoes, oil, and rosemary. Season with kosher salt and pepper and toss to coat evenly. Place the potatoes in the fry basket and insert the fry basket at mid position.
4. Select Air Fry, Convection, and set time to 18 minutes, shaking the basket every 5 minutes and adding the garlic in the last 5 minutes of cooking, or until the fries are golden brown and crisp.
5. Transfer the fries to a plate and sprinkle with flaky sea salt while they're hot. Serve immediately.

Baked Ricotta

Prep time: 10 minutes | Cook time: 15 minutes | Makes 2 cups

- 1 (15-ounce / 425-g) container whole milk Ricotta cheese
- 3 tablespoons grated Parmesan cheese, divided
- 2 tablespoons extra-virgin olive oil
- 1 teaspoon chopped fresh thyme leaves
- 1 teaspoon grated lemon zest
- 1 clove garlic, crushed with press
- ¼ teaspoon salt
- ¼ teaspoon pepper
- Toasted baguette slices or crackers, for serving

1. Press Start/Cancel. Preheat the air fryer oven to 380ºF (193ºC).
2. To get the baking dish in and out of the air fryer oven, create a sling using a 24-inch length of foil, folded lengthwise into thirds.
3. Whisk together the Ricotta, 2 tablespoons of the Parmesan, oil, thyme, lemon zest, garlic, salt, and pepper. Pour into a baking dish. Cover the dish tightly with foil.

4. Place the sling under dish and lift by the ends into the air fryer oven, tucking the ends of the sling around the dish. Insert at low position.
5. Select Bake, Convection, and set time to 10 minutes. Remove the foil cover and sprinkle with the remaining 1 tablespoon of the Parmesan. Bake for 5 more minutes, or until bubbly at edges and the top is browned.
6. Serve warm with toasted baguette slices or crackers.

Lemony Chicken Drumsticks

Prep time: 5 minutes | Cook time: 30 minutes | Serves 2

- 2 teaspoons freshly ground coarse black pepper
- 1 teaspoon baking powder
- ½ teaspoon garlic powder
- 4 chicken drumsticks (4 ounces / 113 g each)
- Kosher salt, to taste
- 1 lemon

1. In a small bowl, stir together the pepper, baking powder, and garlic powder. Place the drumsticks on a plate and sprinkle evenly with the baking powder mixture, turning the drumsticks so they're well coated. Let the drumsticks stand in the refrigerator for at least 1 hour or up to overnight.
2. Press Start/Cancel. Preheat the air fryer oven to 375ºF (191ºC).
3. Sprinkle the drumsticks with salt, then transfer them to the air fryer oven, standing them bone-end up and leaning against the wall of the fry basket. Insert the fry basket at mid position. Select Air Fry, Convection, and set time to 30 minutes, or until cooked through and crisp on the outside.
4. Transfer the drumsticks to a serving platter and finely grate the zest of the lemon over them while they're hot. Cut the lemon into wedges and serve with the warm drumsticks.

Beef and Mango Skewers

Prep time: 10 minutes | Cook time: 5 minutes | Serves 4

- ¾ pound (340 g) beef sirloin tip, cut into 1-inch cubes
- 2 tablespoons balsamic vinegar
- 1 tablespoon olive oil
- 1 tablespoon honey
- ½ teaspoon dried marjoram
- Pinch of salt
- Freshly ground black pepper, to taste
- 1 mango

1. Press Start/Cancel. Preheat the air fryer oven to 390ºF (199ºC).
2. Put the beef cubes in a medium bowl and add the balsamic vinegar, olive oil, honey, marjoram, salt, and pepper. Mix well, then massage the marinade into the beef with your hands. Set aside.
3. To prepare the mango, stand it on end and cut the skin off, using a sharp knife. Then carefully cut around the oval pit to remove the flesh. Cut the mango into 1-inch cubes.
4. Thread metal skewers alternating with three beef cubes and two mango cubes. Place the skewers in the fry basket. Insert at low position.
5. Select Roast, Convection, and set time to 5 minutes, or until the beef is browned and at least 145ºF (63ºC).
6. Serve hot.

Shishito Peppers with Herb Dressing

Prep time: 10 minutes | Cook time: 6 minutes | Serves 2 to 4

- 6 ounces (170 g) shishito peppers
- 1 tablespoon vegetable oil
- Kosher salt and freshly ground black pepper, to taste
- ½ cup mayonnaise
- 2 tablespoons finely chopped fresh basil leaves
- 2 tablespoons finely chopped fresh flat-leaf parsley
- 1 tablespoon finely chopped fresh tarragon
- 1 tablespoon finely chopped fresh chives
- Finely grated zest of ½ lemon
- 1 tablespoon fresh lemon juice
- Flaky sea salt, for serving

1. Press Start/Cancel. Preheat the air fryer oven to 400ºF (204ºC).
2. In a bowl, toss together the shishitos and oil to evenly coat and season with kosher salt and black pepper. Transfer to the fry basket and insert the fry basket at mid position.
3. Select Air Fry, Convection, and set time to 6 minutes, shaking the basket halfway through, or until the shishitos are blistered and lightly charred.
4. Meanwhile, in a small bowl, whisk together the mayonnaise, basil, parsley, tarragon, chives, lemon zest, and lemon juice.
5. Pile the peppers on a plate, sprinkle with flaky sea salt, and serve hot with the dressing.

CHAPTER 4

BREAKFASTS

- 27 Super Easy Bacon Cups
- 27 Classic British Breakfast
- 28 Parmesan Ranch Risotto
- 28 Onion Omelet
- 29 Tomato and Mozzarella Bruschetta
- 29 Potatoes Lyonnaise
- 30 Parmesan Sausage Egg Muffins
- 30 Breakfast Sausage and Cauliflower
- 31 Golden Avocado Tempura
- 31 Egg and Bacon Muffins

Super Easy Bacon Cups

Prep time: 5 minutes | Cook time: 20 minutes | Serves 2

- 3 slices bacon, cooked, sliced in half
- 2 slices ham
- 1 slice tomato
- 2 eggs
- 2 teaspoons grated Parmesan cheese
- Salt and ground black pepper, to taste

1. Press Start/Cancel. Preheat the air fryer oven to 375ºF (191ºC). Line 2 greased muffin tins with 3 half-strips of bacon
2. Put one slice of ham and half slice of tomato in each muffin tin on top of the bacon
3. Crack one egg on top of the tomato in each muffin tin and sprinkle each with half a teaspoon of grated Parmesan cheese. Sprinkle with salt and ground black pepper, if desired.
4. Insert the tin at low position. Select Bake, Convection, and set time to 20 minutes. Remove from the air fryer oven and let cool.
5. Serve warm.

Classic British Breakfast

Prep time: 5 minutes | Cook time: 25 minutes | Serves 2

- 1 cup potatoes, sliced and diced
- 2 cups beans in tomato sauce
- 2 eggs
- 1 tablespoon olive oil
- 1 sausage
- Salt, to taste

1. Press Start/Cancel. Preheat the air fryer oven to 390ºF (199ºC) and allow to warm.
2. Break the eggs onto a baking dish and sprinkle with salt.
3. Lay the beans on the dish, next to the eggs.
4. In a bowl, coat the potatoes with the olive oil. Sprinkle with salt.
5. Transfer the bowl of potato slices to the air fryer oven and insert at low position. Select Bake, Convection, and set time to 10 minutes.
6. Swap out the bowl of potatoes for the dish containing the eggs and beans. Bake for another 10 minutes. Cover the potatoes with parchment paper.
7. Slice up the sausage and throw the slices on top of the beans and eggs. Bake for another 5 minutes.
8. Serve with the potatoes.

Parmesan Ranch Risotto

Prep time: 10 minutes | Cook time: 30 minutes | Serves 2

- 1 tablespoon olive oil
- 1 clove garlic, minced
- 1 tablespoon unsalted butter
- 1 onion, diced
- ¾ cup Arborio rice
- 2 cups chicken stock, boiling
- ½ cup Parmesan cheese, grated

1. Press Start/Cancel. Preheat the air fryer oven to 390ºF (199ºC).
2. Grease a round baking tin with olive oil and stir in the garlic, butter, and onion.
3. Transfer the tin to the air fryer oven and insert at low position. Select Bake, Convection, and set time to 4 minutes. Add the rice and bake for 4 more minutes.
4. Turn the air fryer oven to 320ºF (160ºC) and pour in the chicken stock. Cover and bake for 22 minutes.
5. Scatter with cheese and serve.

Onion Omelet

Prep time: 10 minutes | Cook time: 12 minutes | Serves 2

- 3 eggs
- Salt and ground black pepper, to taste
- ½ teaspoons soy sauce
- 1 large onion, chopped
- 2 tablespoons grated Cheddar cheese
- Cooking spray

1. Press Start/Cancel. Preheat the air fryer oven to 355ºF (179ºC).
2. In a bowl, whisk together the eggs, salt, pepper, and soy sauce.
3. Spritz a small pan with cooking spray. Spread the chopped onion across the bottom of the pan, then transfer the pan to the air fryer oven. Insert at low position.
4. Select Bake, Convection, and set time to 6 minutes, or until the onion is translucent.
5. Add the egg mixture on top of the onions to coat well. Add the cheese on top, then continue baking for another 6 minutes.
6. Allow to cool before serving.

Tomato and Mozzarella Bruschetta

Prep time: 5 minutes | Cook time: 4 minutes | Serves 1

- 6 small loaf slices
- ½ cup tomatoes, finely chopped
- 3 ounces (85 g) Mozzarella cheese, grated
- 1 tablespoon fresh basil, chopped
- 1 tablespoon olive oil

1. Press Start/Cancel. Preheat the air fryer oven to 350ºF (177ºC).
2. Put the loaf slices in the fry basket and insert the fry basket at mid position. Select Air Fry, Convection, and set time to 3 minutes.
3. Add the tomato, Mozzarella, basil, and olive oil on top.
4. Air fry for an additional minute before serving.

Potatoes Lyonnaise

Prep time: 10 minutes | Cook time: 31 minutes | Serves 4

- 1 Vidalia onion, sliced
- 1 teaspoon butter, melted
- 1 teaspoon brown sugar
- 2 large russet potatoes (about 1 pound / 454 g in total), sliced ½-inch thick
- 1 tablespoon vegetable oil
- Salt and freshly ground black pepper, to taste

1. Press Start/Cancel. Preheat the air fryer oven to 370ºF (188ºC).
2. Toss the sliced onions, melted butter and brown sugar together in the fry basket. Insert the fry basket at mid position. Select Air Fry, Convection, and set time to 8 minutes, shaking the basket occasionally to help the onions cook evenly.
3. While the onions are cooking, bring a saucepan of salted water to a boil on the stovetop. Par-cook the potatoes in boiling water for 3 minutes. Drain the potatoes and pat them dry with a clean kitchen towel.
4. Add the potatoes to the onions in the fry basket and drizzle with vegetable oil. Toss to coat the potatoes with the oil and season with salt and freshly ground black pepper.
5. Increase the air fryer oven temperature to 400ºF (204ºC) and air fry for 20 minutes, tossing the vegetables a few times during the cooking time to help the potatoes brown evenly.
6. Season with salt and freshly ground black pepper and serve warm.

Parmesan Sausage Egg Muffins

Prep time: 5 minutes | Cook time: 20 minutes | Serves 4

- 6 ounces (170 g) Italian sausage, sliced
- 6 eggs
- ⅛ cup heavy cream
- Salt and ground black pepper, to taste
- 3 ounces (85 g) Parmesan cheese, grated

1. Press Start/Cancel. Preheat the air fryer oven to 350ºF (177ºC). Grease a muffin pan.
2. Put the sliced sausage in the muffin pan.
3. Beat the eggs with the cream in a bowl and season with salt and pepper.
4. Pour half of the mixture over the sausages in the pan.
5. Sprinkle with cheese and the remaining egg mixture.
6. Insert the pan at low position. Select Bake, Convection, and set time to 20 minutes, or until set.
7. Serve immediately.

Breakfast Sausage and Cauliflower

Prep time: 5 minutes | Cook time: 45 minutes | Serves 4

- 1 pound (454 g) sausage, cooked and crumbled
- 2 cups heavy whipping cream
- 1 head cauliflower, chopped
- 1 cup grated Cheddar cheese, plus more for topping
- 8 eggs, beaten
- Salt and ground black pepper, to taste

1. Press Start/Cancel. Preheat the air fryer oven to 350ºF (177ºC).
2. In a large bowl, mix the sausage, heavy whipping cream, chopped cauliflower, cheese and eggs. Sprinkle with salt and ground black pepper.
3. Pour the mixture into a greased casserole dish. Insert at low position. Select Bake, Convection, and set time to 45 minutes, or until firm.
4. Top with more Cheddar cheese and serve.

Golden Avocado Tempura

Prep time: 5 minutes | Cook time: 10 minutes | Serves 4

- ½ cup bread crumbs
- ½ teaspoons salt
- 1 Haas avocado, pitted, peeled and sliced
- Liquid from 1 can white beans

1. Press Start/Cancel. Preheat the air fryer oven to 350ºF (177ºC).
2. Mix the bread crumbs and salt in a shallow bowl until well-incorporated.
3. Dip the avocado slices in the bean liquid, then into the bread crumbs.
4. Put the avocados in the fry basket, taking care not to overlap any slices. Insert the fry basket at mid position. Select Air Fry, Convection, and set time to 10 minutes. Give the basket a good shake at the halfway point.
5. Serve immediately.

Egg and Bacon Muffins

Prep time: 5 minutes | Cook time: 15 minutes | Serves 1

- 2 eggs
- Salt and ground black pepper, to taste
- 1 tablespoon green pesto
- 3 ounces (85 g) shredded Cheddar cheese
- 5 ounces (142 g) cooked bacon
- 1 scallion, chopped

1. Press Start/Cancel. Preheat the air fryer oven to 350ºF (177ºC). Line a cupcake tin with parchment paper.
2. Beat the eggs with pepper, salt, and pesto in a bowl. Mix in the cheese.
3. Pour the eggs into the cupcake tin and top with the bacon and scallion. Insert the tin at low position.
4. Select Bake, Convection, and set time to 15 minutes, or until the egg is set.
5. Serve immediately.

CHAPTER 5

VEGETABLES AND SIDES

34	Lush Vegetables Roast
34	Potato and Broccoli with Tofu Scramble
35	Ratatouille
35	Roasted Eggplant Slices
36	Super Vegetable Burger
36	Zucchini Balls
37	Cashew Stuffed Mushrooms
37	Crispy Jicama Fries
38	Easy Rosemary Green Beans
38	Roasted Potatoes and Asparagus

Vegetables and Sides|33

Lush Vegetables Roast

Prep time: 15 minutes | Cook time: 20 minutes | Serves 6

- 1 1/3 cups small parsnips, peeled and cubed
- 1 1/3 cups celery
- 2 red onions, sliced
- 1 1/3 cups small butternut squash, cut in half, deseeded and cubed
- 1 tablespoon fresh thyme needles
- 1 tablespoon olive oil
- Salt and ground black pepper, to taste

1. Press Start/Cancel. Preheat the air fryer oven to 390ºF (199ºC).
2. Combine the cut vegetables with the thyme, olive oil, salt and pepper.
3. Put the vegetables in the basket and transfer the basket to the air fryer oven. Insert at low position.
4. Select Roast, Convection, and set time to 20 minutes, stirring once throughout the roasting time, until the vegetables are nicely browned and cooked through.
5. Serve warm.

Potato and Broccoli with Tofu Scramble

Prep time: 15 minutes | Cook time: 30 minutes | Serves 3

- 2½ cups chopped red potato
- 2 tablespoons olive oil, divided
- 1 block tofu, chopped finely
- 2 tablespoons tamari
- 1 teaspoon turmeric powder
- ½ teaspoon onion powder
- ½ teaspoon garlic powder
- ½ cup chopped onion
- 4 cups broccoli florets

1. Press Start/Cancel. Preheat the air fryer oven to 400ºF (204ºC).
2. Toss together the potatoes and 1 tablespoon of the olive oil in a bowl. Transfer to the fry basket. Insert the fry basket at mid position.
3. Select Air Fry, Convection, and set time to 15 minutes, shaking once during the cooking time to ensure they fry evenly.
4. Combine the tofu, the remaining 1 tablespoon of the olive oil, turmeric, onion powder, tamari, and garlic powder together, stirring in the onions, followed by the broccoli.
5. Top the potatoes with the tofu mixture and air fry for an additional 15 minutes. Serve warm.

Ratatouille

Prep time: 20 minutes | Cook time: 25 minutes | Serves 4

- 1 sprig basil
- 1 sprig flat-leaf parsley
- 1 sprig mint
- 1 tablespoon coriander powder
- 1 teaspoon capers
- ½ lemon, juiced
- Salt and ground black pepper, to taste
- 2 eggplants, sliced crosswise
- 2 red onions, chopped
- 4 cloves garlic, minced
- 2 red peppers, sliced crosswise
- 1 fennel bulb, sliced crosswise
- 3 large zucchinis, sliced crosswise
- 5 tablespoons olive oil
- 4 large tomatoes, chopped
- 2 teaspoons herbs de Provence

1. Blend the basil, parsley, coriander, mint, lemon juice and capers, with a little salt and pepper. Make sure all ingredients are well-incorporated.
2. Press Start/Cancel. Preheat the air fryer oven to 400ºF (204ºC).
3. Coat the eggplant, onions, garlic, peppers, fennel, and zucchini with olive oil.
4. Transfer the vegetables into a baking dish and top with the tomatoes and herb purée. Sprinkle with more salt and pepper, and the herbs de Provence.
5. Insert the baking dish at mid position. Select Air Fry, Convection, and set time to 25 minutes.
6. Serve immediately.

Roasted Eggplant Slices

Prep time: 5 minutes | Cook time: 15 minutes | Serves 1

- 1 large eggplant, sliced
- 2 tablespoons olive oil
- ¼ teaspoon salt
- ½ teaspoon garlic powder

1. Press Start/Cancel. Preheat the air fryer oven to 390ºF (199ºC).
2. Apply the olive oil to the slices with a brush, coating both sides. Season each side with sprinklings of salt and garlic powder. Place the slices in the food tray. Insert at low position.
3. Select Roast, Convection, and set time to 15 minutes.
4. Serve immediately.

Super Vegetable Burger

Prep time: 15 minutes | Cook time: 12 minutes | Serves 8

- ½ pound (227 g) cauliflower, steamed and diced, rinsed and drained
- 2 teaspoons coconut oil, melted
- 2 teaspoons minced garlic
- ¼ cup desiccated coconut
- ½ cup oats
- 3 tablespoons flour
- 1 tablespoon flaxseeds plus 3 tablespoons water, divided
- 1 teaspoon mustard powder
- 2 teaspoons thyme
- 2 teaspoons parsley
- 2 teaspoons chives
- Salt and ground black pepper, to taste
- 1 cup bread crumbs

1. Press Start/Cancel. Preheat the air fryer oven to 390ºF (199ºC).
2. Combine the cauliflower with all the ingredients, except for the bread crumbs, incorporating everything well.
3. Using the hands, shape 8 equal-sized amounts of the mixture into burger patties. Coat the patties in bread crumbs before putting them in the fry basket in a single layer. Insert the fry basket at mid position.
4. Select Air Fry, Convection, and set time to 12 minutes or until crispy.
5. Serve hot.

Zucchini Balls

Prep time: 5 minutes | Cook time: 10 minutes | Serves 4

- 4 zucchinis
- 1 egg
- ½ cup grated Parmesan cheese
- 1 tablespoon Italian herbs
- 1 cup grated coconut

1. Thinly grate the zucchinis and dry with a cheesecloth, ensuring to remove all the moisture.
2. In a bowl, combine the zucchinis with the egg, Parmesan, Italian herbs, and grated coconut, mixing well to incorporate everything. Using the hands, mold the mixture into balls.
3. Press Start/Cancel. Preheat the air fryer oven to 400ºF (204ºC).
4. Lay the zucchini balls in the fry basket and insert the fry basket at mid position. Select Air Fry, Convection, and set time to 10 minutes.
5. Serve hot.

Cashew Stuffed Mushrooms

Prep time: 10 minutes | Cook time: 15 minutes | Serves 6

- 1 cup basil
- ½ cup cashew, soaked overnight
- ½ cup nutritional yeast
- 1 tablespoon lemon juice
- 2 cloves garlic
- 1 tablespoon olive oil
- Salt, to taste
- 1 pound (454 g) baby Bella mushroom, stems removed

1. Press Start/Cancel. Preheat the air fryer oven to 400ºF (204ºC).
2. Prepare the pesto. In a food processor, blend the basil, cashew nuts, nutritional yeast, lemon juice, garlic and olive oil to combine well. Sprinkle with salt as desired.
3. Turn the mushrooms cap-side down and spread the pesto on the underside of each cap.
4. Transfer to the fry basket and insert the fry basket at mid position. Select Air Fry, Convection, and set time to 15 minutes.
5. Serve warm.

Crispy Jicama Fries

Prep time: 5 minutes | Cook time: 20 minutes | Serves 1

- 1 small jicama, peeled
- ¼ teaspoon onion powder
- ¾ teaspoon chili powder
- ¼ teaspoon garlic powder
- ¼ teaspoon ground black pepper

1. Press Start/Cancel. Preheat the air fryer oven to 350ºF (177ºC).
2. To make the fries, cut the jicama into matchsticks of the desired thickness.
3. In a bowl, toss them with the onion powder, chili powder, garlic powder, and black pepper to coat. Transfer the fries into the fry basket. Insert the fry basket at mid position.
4. Select Air Fry, Convection, and set time to 20 minutes, giving the basket an occasional shake throughout the cooking process. The fries are ready when they are hot and golden.
5. Serve immediately.

Easy Rosemary Green Beans

Prep time: 5 minutes | Cook time: 5 minutes | Serves 1

- 1 tablespoon butter, melted
- 2 tablespoons rosemary
- ½ teaspoon salt
- 3 cloves garlic, minced
- ¾ cup chopped green beans

1. Press Start/Cancel. Preheat the air fryer oven to 390ºF (199ºC).
2. In a bowl, combine the melted butter with the rosemary, salt, and minced garlic. Toss in the green beans, coating them well. Transfer to the fry basket. Insert the fry basket at mid position.
3. Select Air Fry, Convection, and set time to 5 minutes.
4. Serve immediately.

Roasted Potatoes and Asparagus

Prep time: 5 minutes | Cook time: 23 minutes | Serves 4

- 4 medium potatoes
- 1 bunch asparagus
- ⅓ cup cottage cheese
- ⅓ cup low-fat crème fraiche
- 1 tablespoon wholegrain mustard
- Salt and pepper, to taste
- Cook spray

1. Press Start/Cancel. Preheat the air fryer oven to 390ºF (199ºC). Spritz the fry basket with cooking spray.
2. Place the potatoes in the basket. Insert the fry basket at mid position. Select Air Fry, Convection, and set time to 20 minutes.
3. Boil the asparagus in salted water for 3 minutes.
4. Remove the potatoes and mash them with rest of ingredients. Sprinkle with salt and pepper.
5. Serve immediately.

CHAPTER 6

WRAPS AND SANDWICHES

41	Veggie Salsa Wraps
41	Tuna Muffin Sandwich
42	Tuna and Lettuce Wraps
42	Chicken Pita Sandwich
43	Nugget and Veggie Taco Wraps
43	Cheesy Chicken Sandwich
44	Cheesy Greens Sandwich
44	Classic Sloppy Joes
45	Smoky Chicken Sandwich
46	Chicken-Lettuce Wraps

Veggie Salsa Wraps

Prep time: 5 minutes | Cook time: 7 minutes | Serves 4

- 1 cup red onion, sliced
- 1 zucchini, chopped
- 1 poblano pepper, deseeded and finely chopped
- 1 head lettuce
- ½ cup salsa
- 8 ounces (227 g) Mozzarella cheese

1. Press Start/Cancel. Preheat the air fryer oven to 390ºF (199ºC).
2. Place the red onion, zucchini, and poblano pepper in the fry basket and insert the fry basket at mid position. Select Air Fry, Convection, and set time to 7 minutes, or until they are tender and fragrant.
3. Divide the veggie mixture among the lettuce leaves and spoon the salsa over the top. Finish off with Mozzarella cheese. Wrap the lettuce leaves around the filling.
4. Serve immediately.

Tuna Muffin Sandwich

Prep time: 8 minutes | Cook time: 6 minutes | Serves 4

- 1 (6-ounce / 170-g) can chunk light tuna, drained
- ¼ cup mayonnaise
- 2 tablespoons mustard
- 1 tablespoon lemon juice
- 2 green onions, minced
- 3 English muffins, split with a fork
- 3 tablespoons softened butter
- 6 thin slices Provolone or Muenster cheese

1. Press Start/Cancel. Preheat the air fryer oven to 390ºF (199ºC).
2. In a small bowl, combine the tuna, mayonnaise, mustard, lemon juice, and green onions. Set aside.
3. Butter the cut side of the English muffins. Place the the muffins in the fry basket, butter-side up. Insert at low position.
4. Select Bake, Convection, and set time to 3 minutes, or until light golden brown. Remove the muffins from the fry basket.
5. Top each muffin with one slice of cheese and return to the air fryer oven. Bake for 3 minutes or until the cheese melts and starts to brown.
6. Remove the muffins from the air fryer oven, top with the tuna mixture, and serve.

Tuna and Lettuce Wraps

Prep time: 10 minutes | Cook time: 5 minutes | Serves 4

- 1 pound (454 g) fresh tuna steak, cut into 1-inch cubes
- 1 tablespoon grated fresh ginger
- 2 garlic cloves, minced
- ½ teaspoon toasted sesame oil
- 4 low-sodium whole-wheat tortillas
- ¼ cup low-fat mayonnaise
- 2 cups shredded romaine lettuce
- 1 red bell pepper, thinly sliced

1. Press Start/Cancel. Preheat the air fryer oven to 390ºF (199ºC).
2. In a medium bowl, mix the tuna, ginger, garlic, and sesame oil. Let it stand for 10 minutes. Transfer to the fry basket. Insert the fry basket at mid position.
3. Select Air Fry, Convection, and set time to 5 minutes, or until lightly browned.
4. Make the wraps with the tuna, tortillas, mayonnaise, lettuce, and bell pepper.
5. Serve immediately.

Chicken Pita Sandwich

Prep time: 10 minutes | Cook time: 10 minutes | Serves 4

- 2 boneless, skinless chicken breasts, cut into 1-inch cubes
- 1 small red onion, sliced
- 1 red bell pepper, sliced
- ⅓ cup Italian salad dressing, divided
- ½ teaspoon dried thyme
- 4 pita pockets, split
- 2 cups torn butter lettuce
- 1 cup chopped cherry tomatoes

1. Press Start/Cancel. Preheat the air fryer oven to 380ºF (193ºC).
2. Place the chicken, onion, and bell pepper in the fry basket. Drizzle with 1 tablespoon of the Italian salad dressing, add the thyme, and toss. Insert at low position.
3. Select Bake, Convection, and set time to 10 minutes, or until the chicken is 165ºF (74ºC) on a food thermometer, stirring once during cooking time.
4. Transfer the chicken and vegetables to a bowl and toss with the remaining salad dressing.
5. Assemble sandwiches with the pita pockets, butter lettuce, and cherry tomatoes. Serve immediately.

Nugget and Veggie Taco Wraps

Prep time: 5 minutes | Cook time: 15 minutes | Serves 4

- 1 tablespoon water
- 4 pieces commercial vegan nuggets, chopped
- 1 small yellow onion, diced
- 1 small red bell pepper, chopped
- 2 cobs grilled corn kernels
- 4 large corn tortillas
- Mixed greens, for garnish

1. Press Start/Cancel. Preheat the air fryer oven to 400ºF (204ºC).
2. Over a medium heat, sauté the nuggets in the water with the onion, corn kernels and bell pepper in a skillet, then remove from the heat.
3. Fill the tortillas with the nuggets and vegetables and fold them up. Transfer to the fry basket and insert the fry basket at mid position. Select Air Fry, Convection, and set time to 15 minutes.
4. Once crispy, serve immediately, garnished with the mixed greens.

Cheesy Chicken Sandwich

Prep time: 10 minutes | Cook time: 6 minutes | Serves 1

- $1/3$ cup chicken, cooked and shredded
- 2 Mozzarella slices
- 1 hamburger bun
- ¼ cup shredded cabbage
- 1 teaspoon mayonnaise
- 2 teaspoons butter, melted
- 1 teaspoon olive oil
- ½ teaspoon balsamic vinegar
- ¼ teaspoon smoked paprika
- ¼ teaspoon black pepper
- ¼ teaspoon garlic powder
- Pinch of salt

1. Press Start/Cancel. Preheat the air fryer oven to 370ºF (188ºC).
2. Brush some butter onto the outside of the hamburger bun.
3. In a bowl, coat the chicken with the garlic powder, salt, pepper, and paprika.
4. In a separate bowl, stir together the mayonnaise, olive oil, cabbage, and balsamic vinegar to make coleslaw.
5. Slice the bun in two. Start building the sandwich, starting with the chicken, followed by the Mozzarella, the coleslaw, and finally the top bun.
6. Transfer the sandwich to the air fryer oven and insert at low position. Select Bake, Convection, and set time to 6 minutes.
7. Serve immediately.

Cheesy Greens Sandwich

Prep time: 15 minutes | Cook time: 12 minutes | Serves 4

- 1½ cups chopped mixed greens
- 2 garlic cloves, thinly sliced
- 2 teaspoons olive oil
- 2 slices low-sodium low-fat Swiss cheese
- 4 slices low-sodium whole-wheat bread
- Cooking spray

1. Press Start/Cancel. Preheat the air fryer oven to 400ºF (204ºC).
2. In a baking pan, mix the greens, garlic, and olive oil. Insert at mid position. Select Air Fry, Convection, and set time to 5 minutes, stirring once, until the vegetables are tender. Drain, if necessary.
3. Make 2 sandwiches, dividing half of the greens and 1 slice of Swiss cheese between 2 slices of bread. Place the sandwiches in the food tray. Lightly spray the outsides of the sandwiches with cooking spray. Insert at low position.
4. Select Bake, Convection, and set time to 7 minutes, turning with tongs halfway through, until the bread is toasted and the cheese melts.
5. Cut each sandwich in half and serve.

Classic Sloppy Joes

Prep time: 10 minutes | Cook time: 18 minutes | Makes 4 large sandwiches or 8 sliders

- 1 pound (454 g) very lean ground beef
- 1 teaspoon onion powder
- ⅓ cup ketchup
- ¼ cup water
- ½ teaspoon celery seed
- 1 tablespoon lemon juice
- 1½ teaspoons brown sugar
- 1¼ teaspoons low-sodium Worcestershire sauce
- ½ teaspoon salt (optional)
- ½ teaspoon vinegar
- ⅛ teaspoon dry mustard
- Hamburger or slider buns, for serving
- Cooking spray

1. Press Start/Cancel. Preheat the air fryer oven to 330ºF (166ºC). Spray the fry basket with cooking spray.
2. Break raw ground beef into small chunks and pile into the basket. Insert at low position. Select Roast, Convection, and set time to 5 minutes. Stir to break apart and roast for 3 minutes. Stir and roast for 3 minutes longer, or until meat is well done.

3. Remove the meat from the air fryer oven, drain, and use a knife and fork to crumble into small pieces.
4. Give your fry basket a quick rinse to remove any bits of meat.
5. Place all the remaining ingredients, except for the buns, in a baking pan and mix together. Add the meat and stir well. Insert at low position.
6. Select Bake, Convection, and set time to 5 minutes. Stir and bake for 2 minutes.
7. Scoop onto buns. Serve hot.

Smoky Chicken Sandwich

Prep time: 10 minutes | Cook time: 11 minutes | Serves 2

- 2 boneless, skinless chicken breasts (8 ounces / 227 g each), sliced horizontally in half and separated into 4 thinner cutlets
- Kosher salt and freshly ground black pepper, to taste
- ½ cup all-purpose flour
- 3 large eggs, lightly beaten
- ½ cup dried bread crumbs
- 1 tablespoon smoked paprika
- Cooking spray
- ½ cup marinara sauce
- 6 ounces (170 g) smoked Mozzarella cheese, grated
- 2 store-bought soft, sesame-seed hamburger or Italian buns, split

1. Press Start/Cancel. Preheat the air fryer oven to 350ºF (177ºC).
2. Season the chicken cutlets all over with salt and pepper. Set up three shallow bowls: Place the flour in the first bowl, the eggs in the second, and stir together the bread crumbs and smoked paprika in the third. Coat the chicken pieces in the flour, then dip fully in the egg. Dredge in the paprika bread crumbs, then transfer to a wire rack set over a baking sheet and spray both sides liberally with cooking spray.
3. Transfer 2 of the chicken cutlets to the fry basket and insert the fry basket at mid position. Select Air Fry, Convection, and set time to 6 minutes, or until beginning to brown. Spread each cutlet with 2 tablespoons of the marinara sauce and sprinkle with one-quarter of the smoked Mozzarella. Increase the temperature to 400ºF (204ºC) and air fry for 5 minutes more, or until the chicken is cooked through and crisp and the cheese is melted and golden brown.
4. Transfer the cutlets to a plate, stack on top of each other, and place inside a bun. Repeat with the remaining chicken cutlets, marinara, smoked Mozzarella, and bun.
5. Serve the sandwiches warm.

Chicken-Lettuce Wraps

Prep time: 15 minutes | Cook time: 14 minutes | Serves 2 to 4

- 1 pound (454 g) boneless, skinless chicken thighs, trimmed
- 1 teaspoon vegetable oil
- 2 tablespoons lime juice
- 1 shallot, minced
- 1 tablespoon fish sauce, plus extra for serving
- 2 teaspoons packed brown sugar
- 1 garlic clove, minced
- ⅛ teaspoon red pepper flakes
- 1 mango, peeled, pitted, and cut into ¼-inch pieces
- ⅓ cup chopped fresh mint
- ⅓ cup chopped fresh cilantro
- ⅓ cup chopped fresh Thai basil
- 1 head Bibb lettuce, leaves separated (8 ounces / 227 g)
- ¼ cup chopped dry-roasted peanuts
- 2 Thai chiles, stemmed and sliced thin

1. Press Start/Cancel. Preheat the air fryer oven to 400ºF (204ºC).
2. Pat the chicken dry with paper towels and rub with oil. Place the chicken in fry basket and insert the fry basket at mid position.
3. Select Air Fry, Convection, and set time to 14 minutes, or until the chicken registers 175ºF (79ºC), flipping and rotating chicken halfway through cooking.
4. Meanwhile, whisk lime juice, shallot, fish sauce, sugar, garlic, and pepper flakes together in large bowl; set aside.
5. Transfer chicken to cutting board, let cool slightly, then shred into bite-size pieces using 2 forks. Add the shredded chicken, mango, mint, cilantro, and basil to bowl with dressing and toss to coat.
6. Serve the chicken in the lettuce leaves, passing peanuts, Thai chiles, and extra fish sauce separately.

CHAPTER 7

POULTRY

49	Lemon Chicken and Spinach Salad
49	Cranberry Curry Chicken
50	Jerk Chicken Leg Quarters
50	Tex-Mex Chicken Breasts
51	Apricot Glazed Turkey Tenderloin
51	Turkey and Cranberry Quesadillas
52	Almond-Crusted Chicken Nuggets
52	Lemon Garlic Chicken
53	Curried Orange Honey Chicken
53	Chicken with Pineapple and Peach
54	Pecan-Crusted Turkey Cutlets

Lemon Chicken and Spinach Salad

Prep time: 10 minutes | Cook time: 16 to 20 minutes | Serves 4

- 3 (5-ounce / 142-g) low-sodium boneless, skinless chicken breasts, cut into 1-inch cubes
- 5 teaspoons olive oil
- ½ teaspoon dried thyme
- 1 medium red onion, sliced
- 1 red bell pepper, sliced
- 1 small zucchini, cut into strips
- 3 tablespoons freshly squeezed lemon juice
- 6 cups fresh baby spinach

1. Press Start/Cancel. Preheat the air fryer oven to 400ºF (204ºC).
2. In a large bowl, mix the chicken with the olive oil and thyme. Toss to coat. Transfer to a medium metal bowl and insert at low position. Select Roast, Convection, and set time to 8 minutes.
3. Add the red onion, red bell pepper, and zucchini. Roast for 8 to 12 minutes more, stirring once during cooking, or until the chicken reaches an internal temperature of 165ºF (74ºC) on a meat thermometer.
4. Remove the bowl from the air fryer oven and stir in the lemon juice.
5. Put the spinach in a serving bowl and top with the chicken mixture. Toss to combine and serve immediately.

Cranberry Curry Chicken

Prep time: 12 minutes | Cook time: 18 minutes | Serves 4

- 3 (5-ounce / 142-g) low-sodium boneless, skinless chicken breasts, cut into 1½-inch cubes
- 2 teaspoons olive oil
- 2 tablespoons cornstarch
- 1 tablespoon curry powder
- 1 tart apple, chopped
- ½ cup low-sodium chicken broth
- ⅓ cup dried cranberries
- 2 tablespoons freshly squeezed orange juice
- Brown rice, cooked (optional)

1. Press Start/Cancel. Preheat the air fryer oven to 380ºF (193ºC).
2. In a medium bowl, mix the chicken and olive oil. Sprinkle with the cornstarch and curry powder. Toss to coat. Stir in the apple and transfer to a metal pan. Insert the pan at low position. Select Bake, Convection, and set time to 8 minutes, stirring once during cooking.
3. Add the chicken broth, cranberries, and orange juice. Bake for about 10 minutes more, or until the sauce is slightly thickened and the chicken reaches an internal temperature of 165ºF (74ºC) on a meat thermometer. Serve over hot cooked brown rice, if desired.

Jerk Chicken Leg Quarters

Prep time: 8 minutes | Cook time: 28 minutes | Serves 2

- 1 tablespoon packed brown sugar
- 1 teaspoon ground allspice
- 1 teaspoon pepper
- 1 teaspoon garlic powder
- ¾ teaspoon dry mustard
- ¾ teaspoon dried thyme
- ½ teaspoon salt
- ¼ teaspoon cayenne pepper
- 2 (10-ounce / 284-g) chicken leg quarters, trimmed
- 1 teaspoon vegetable oil
- 1 scallion, green part only, sliced thin
- Lime wedges

1. Press Start/Cancel. Preheat the air fryer oven to 400ºF (204ºC).
2. Combine sugar, allspice, pepper, garlic powder, mustard, thyme, salt, and cayenne in a bowl. Pat chicken dry with paper towels. Using metal skewer, poke 10 to 15 holes in skin of each chicken leg. Rub with oil and sprinkle evenly with spice mixture.
3. Arrange chicken skin-side up in the fry basket, spaced evenly apart. Insert the fry basket at mid position. Select Air Fry, Convection, and set time to 28 minutes, or until chicken is well browned and crisp, rotating chicken halfway through cooking (do not flip).
4. Transfer chicken to plate, tent loosely with aluminum foil, and let rest for 5 minutes. Sprinkle with scallion. Serve with lime wedges.

Tex-Mex Chicken Breasts

Prep time: 10 minutes | Cook time: 18 minutes | Serves 4

- 1 pound (454 g) low-sodium boneless, skinless chicken breasts, cut into 1-inch cubes
- 1 medium onion, chopped
- 1 red bell pepper, chopped
- 1 jalapeño pepper, minced
- 2 teaspoons olive oil
- ⅔ cup canned low-sodium black beans, rinsed and drained
- ½ cup low-sodium salsa
- 2 teaspoons chili powder

1. Press Start/Cancel. Preheat the air fryer oven to 400ºF (204ºC).
2. In a medium metal bowl, mix the chicken, onion, bell pepper, jalapeño, and olive oil. Insert at low position. Select Roast, Convection, and set time to 10 minutes, stirring once during cooking.
3. Add the black beans, salsa, and chili powder. Roast for 8 minutes more, stirring once, until the chicken reaches an internal temperature of 165ºF (74ºC) on a meat thermometer. Serve immediately.

Apricot Glazed Turkey Tenderloin

Prep time: 20 minutes | Cook time: 28 minutes | Serves 4

- ¼ cup sugar-free apricot preserves
- ½ tablespoon spicy brown mustard
- 1½ pounds (680 g) turkey breast tenderloin
- Salt and freshly ground black pepper, to taste
- Olive oil spray

1. Press Start/Cancel. Preheat the air fryer oven to 370°F (188°C). Spray the fry basket lightly with olive oil spray.
2. In a small bowl, combine the apricot preserves and mustard to make a paste.
3. Season the turkey with salt and pepper. Spread the apricot paste all over the turkey.
4. Place the turkey in the fry basket and lightly spray with olive oil spray.
5. Insert the fry basket at mid position. Select Air Fry, Convection, and set time to 15 minutes. Flip the turkey over and lightly spray with olive oil spray. Air fry until the internal temperature reaches at least 170°F (77°C), an additional 13 minutes.
6. Let the turkey rest for 10 minutes before slicing and serving.

Turkey and Cranberry Quesadillas

Prep time: 7 minutes | Cook time: 4 to 8 minutes | Serves 4

- 6 low-sodium whole-wheat tortillas
- ⅓ cup shredded low-sodium low-fat Swiss cheese
- ¾ cup shredded cooked low-sodium turkey breast
- 2 tablespoons cranberry sauce
- 2 tablespoons dried cranberries
- ½ teaspoon dried basil
- Olive oil spray, for spraying the tortillas

1. Press Start/Cancel. Preheat the air fryer oven to 400°F (204°C).
2. Put 3 tortillas on a work surface.
3. Evenly divide the Swiss cheese, turkey, cranberry sauce, and dried cranberries among the tortillas. Sprinkle with the basil and top with the remaining tortillas.
4. Spray the outsides of the tortillas with olive oil spray and transfer to the fry basket. Insert the fry basket at mid position. Select Air Fry, Convection, and set time to 6 minutes, or until crisp and the cheese is melted. Cut into quarters and serve.

Almond-Crusted Chicken Nuggets

Prep time: 10 minutes | Cook time: 12 minutes | Serves 4

- 1 egg white
- 1 tablespoon freshly squeezed lemon juice
- ½ teaspoon dried basil
- ½ teaspoon ground paprika
- 1 pound (454 g) low-sodium boneless, skinless chicken breasts, cut into 1½-inch cubes
- ½ cup ground almonds
- 2 slices low-sodium whole-wheat bread, crumbled

1. Press Start/Cancel. Preheat the air fryer oven to 400ºF (204ºC).
2. In a shallow bowl, beat the egg white, lemon juice, basil, and paprika with a fork until foamy.
3. Add the chicken and stir to coat.
4. On a plate, mix the almonds and bread crumbs.
5. Toss the chicken cubes in the almond and bread crumb mixture until coated.
6. Place the nuggets in the fry basket. Insert the basket at low position.
7. Select Bake, Convection, and set time to 12 minutes, or until the chicken reaches an internal temperature of 165ºF (74ºC) on a meat thermometer. You may need to work in batches.
8. Serve immediately.

Lemon Garlic Chicken

Prep time: 10 minutes | Cook time: 18 minutes | Serves 4

- 4 (5-ounce / 142-g) low-sodium boneless, skinless chicken breasts, cut into 4-by-½-inch strips
- 2 teaspoons olive oil
- 2 tablespoons cornstarch
- 3 garlic cloves, minced
- ½ cup low-sodium chicken broth
- ¼ cup freshly squeezed lemon juice
- 1 tablespoon honey
- ½ teaspoon dried thyme
- Brown rice, cooked (optional)

1. Press Start/Cancel. Preheat the air fryer oven to 400ºF (204ºC).
2. In a large bowl, mix the chicken and olive oil. Sprinkle with the cornstarch. Toss to coat.
3. Add the garlic and transfer to a metal pan. Insert the pan at low position. Select Bake, Convection, and set time to 10 minutes, stirring once during cooking.
4. Add the chicken broth, lemon juice, honey, and thyme to the chicken mixture. Bake for 8 minutes more, or until the sauce is slightly thickened and the chicken reaches an internal temperature of 165ºF (74ºC) on a meat thermometer.
5. Serve over hot cooked brown rice, if desired.

Curried Orange Honey Chicken

Prep time: 10 minutes | Cook time: 17 minutes | Serves 4

- ¾ pound (340 g) boneless, skinless chicken thighs, cut into 1-inch pieces
- 1 yellow bell pepper, cut into 1½-inch pieces
- 1 small red onion, sliced
- Olive oil for misting
- ¼ cup chicken stock
- 2 tablespoons honey
- ¼ cup orange juice
- 1 tablespoon cornstarch
- 2 to 3 teaspoons curry powder

1. Press Start/Cancel. Preheat the air fryer oven to 370ºF (188ºC).
2. Put the chicken thighs, pepper, and red onion in the fry basket and mist with olive oil. Insert at low position.
3. Select Roast, Convection, and set time to 13 minutes, or until the chicken is cooked to 165ºF (74ºC), shaking the basket halfway through cooking time.
4. Remove the chicken and vegetables from the fry basket and set aside.
5. In a metal bowl, combine the stock, honey, orange juice, cornstarch, and curry powder, and mix well. Add the chicken and vegetables, stir, and put the bowl in the basket.
6. Return the basket to the air fryer oven and roast for 2 minutes. Remove and stir, then roast for 2 minutes or until the sauce is thickened and bubbly.
7. Serve warm.

Chicken with Pineapple and Peach

Prep time: 10 minutes | Cook time: 15 minutes | Serves 4

- 1 pound (454 g) low-sodium boneless, skinless chicken breasts, cut into 1-inch pieces
- 1 medium red onion, chopped
- 1 (8-ounce / 227-g) can pineapple chunks, drained, ¼ cup juice reserved
- 1 tablespoon peanut oil or safflower oil
- 1 peach, peeled, pitted, and cubed
- 1 tablespoon cornstarch
- ½ teaspoon ground ginger
- ¼ teaspoon ground allspice
- Brown rice, cooked (optional)

1. Press Start/Cancel. Preheat the air fryer oven to 380ºF (193ºC).
2. In a medium metal bowl, mix the chicken, red onion, pineapple, and peanut oil. Insert the bowl at low position. Select Bake, Convection, and set time to 9 minutes. Remove and stir.

3. Add the peach and return the bowl to the air fryer oven. Bake for 3 minutes more. Remove and stir again.
4. In a small bowl, whisk the reserved pineapple juice, the cornstarch, ginger, and allspice well. Add to the chicken mixture and stir to combine.
5. Bake for 3 minutes more, or until the chicken reaches an internal temperature of 165°F (74°C) on a meat thermometer and the sauce is slightly thickened.
6. Serve immediately over hot cooked brown rice, if desired.

Pecan-Crusted Turkey Cutlets

Prep time: 10 minutes | Cook time: 11 minutes | Serves 4

- ¾ cup panko bread crumbs
- ¼ teaspoon salt
- ¼ teaspoon pepper
- ¼ teaspoon dry mustard
- ¼ teaspoon poultry seasoning
- ½ cup pecans
- ¼ cup cornstarch
- 1 egg, beaten
- 1 pound (454 g) turkey cutlets, ½-inch thick
- Salt and pepper, to taste
- Cooking spray

1. Press Start/Cancel. Preheat the air fryer oven to 360°F (182°C).
2. Place the panko crumbs, salt, pepper, mustard, and poultry seasoning in a food processor. Process until crumbs are finely crushed. Add pecans and process just until nuts are finely chopped.
3. Place cornstarch in a shallow dish and beaten egg in another. Transfer coating mixture from food processor into a third shallow dish.
4. Sprinkle turkey cutlets with salt and pepper to taste.
5. Dip cutlets in cornstarch and shake off excess, then dip in beaten egg and finally roll in crumbs, pressing to coat well. Spray both sides with cooking spray.
6. Place 2 cutlets in fry basket in a single layer and insert the fry basket at mid position. Select Air Fry, Convection, and set time to 11 minutes. Repeat with the remaining cutlets.
7. Serve warm.

CHAPTER 8

MEATS

57 Greek Lamb Rack
57 Italian Lamb Chops with Avocado Mayo
58 Beef and Pork Sausage Meatloaf
58 Beef and Spinach Rolls
59 Beef Chuck Cheeseburgers
59 Kale and Beef Omelet
60 BBQ Pork Steaks
60 Pork Medallions with Radicchio and Endive Salad
61 Beef Chuck with Brussels Sprouts
62 Sun-dried Tomato Crusted Chops
63 Bacon and Pear Stuffed Pork Chops
64 Spinach and Beef Braciole

Greek Lamb Rack

Prep time: 5 minutes | Cook time: 10 minutes | Serves 4

- ¼ cup freshly squeezed lemon juice
- 1 teaspoon oregano
- 2 teaspoons minced fresh rosemary
- 1 teaspoon minced fresh thyme
- 2 tablespoons minced garlic
- Salt and freshly ground black pepper, to taste
- 2 to 4 tablespoons olive oil
- 1 lamb rib rack (7 to 8 ribs)

1. Press Start/Cancel. Preheat the air fryer oven to 360ºF (182ºC).
2. In a small mixing bowl, combine the lemon juice, oregano, rosemary, thyme, garlic, salt, pepper, and olive oil and mix well.
3. Rub the mixture over the lamb, covering all the meat. Put the rack of lamb in the food tray. Insert at low position. Select Roast, Convection, and set time to 10 minutes. Flip the rack halfway through.
4. After 10 minutes, measure the internal temperature of the rack of lamb reaches at least 145ºF (63ºC).
5. Serve immediately.

Italian Lamb Chops with Avocado Mayo

Prep time: 5 minutes | Cook time: 12 minutes | Serves 2

- 2 lamp chops
- 2 teaspoons Italian herbs
- 2 avocados
- ½ cup mayonnaise
- 1 tablespoon lemon juice

1. Season the lamb chops with the Italian herbs, then set aside for 5 minutes.
2. Press Start/Cancel. Preheat the air fryer oven to 400ºF (204ºC) and place the fry basket inside.
3. Put the chops in the fry basket and insert at mid position. Select Air Fry, Convection, and set time to 12 minutes.
4. In the meantime, halve the avocados and open to remove the pits. Spoon the flesh into a blender.
5. Add the mayonnaise and lemon juice and pulse until a smooth consistency is achieved.
6. Take care when removing the chops from the air fryer oven, then plate up and serve with the avocado mayo.

Beef and Pork Sausage Meatloaf

Prep time: 20 minutes | Cook time: 25 minutes | Serves 4

- ¾ pound (340 g) ground chuck
- 4 ounces (113 g) ground pork sausage
- 1 cup shallots, finely chopped
- 2 eggs, well beaten
- 3 tablespoons plain milk
- 1 tablespoon oyster sauce
- 1 teaspoon porcini mushrooms
- ½ teaspoon cumin powder
- 1 teaspoon garlic paste
- 1 tablespoon fresh parsley
- Salt and crushed red pepper flakes, to taste
- 1 cup crushed saltines
- Cooking spray

1. Press Start/Cancel. Preheat the air fryer oven to 360ºF (182ºC). Spritz a baking dish with cooking spray.
2. Mix all the ingredients in a large bowl, combining everything well.
3. Transfer to the baking dish and insert at low position. Select Bake, Convection, and set time to 25 minutes.
4. Serve hot.

Beef and Spinach Rolls

Prep time: 10 minutes | Cook time: 14 minutes | Serves 2

- 3 teaspoons pesto
- 2 pounds (907 g) beef flank steak
- 6 slices provolone cheese
- 3 ounces (85 g) roasted red bell peppers
- ¾ cup baby spinach
- 1 teaspoon sea salt
- 1 teaspoon black pepper

1. Press Start/Cancel. Preheat the air fryer oven to 400ºF (204ºC).
2. Spoon equal amounts of the pesto onto each flank steak and spread it across evenly.
3. Put the cheese, roasted red peppers and spinach on top of the meat, about three-quarters of the way down.
4. Roll the steak up, holding it in place with toothpicks. Sprinkle with the sea salt and pepper.
5. Put inside the fry basket and insert the fry basket at mid position. Select Air Fry, Convection, and set time to 14 minutes, turning halfway through the cooking time.
6. Allow the beef to rest for 10 minutes before slicing up and serving.

Beef Chuck Cheeseburgers

Prep time: 10 minutes | Cook time: 11 minutes | Serves 4

- ¾ pound (340 g) ground beef chuck
- 1 envelope onion soup mix
- Kosher salt and freshly ground black pepper, to taste
- 1 teaspoon paprika
- 4 slices Monterey Jack cheese
- 4 ciabatta rolls

1. In a bowl, stir together the ground chuck, onion soup mix, salt, black pepper, and paprika to combine well.
2. Press Start/Cancel. Preheat the air fryer oven to 385ºF (196ºC).
3. Take four equal portions of the mixture and mold each one into a patty. Transfer to the fry basket and insert the fry basket at mid position. Select Air Fry, Convection, and set time to 10 minutes.
4. Put the slices of cheese on the top of the burgers.
5. Air fry for another minute before serving on ciabatta rolls.

Kale and Beef Omelet

Prep time: 15 minutes | Cook time: 16 minutes | Serves 4

- ½ pound (227 g) leftover beef, coarsely chopped
- 2 garlic cloves, pressed
- 1 cup kale, torn into pieces and wilted
- 1 tomato, chopped
- ¼ teaspoon sugar
- 4 eggs, beaten
- 4 tablespoons heavy cream
- ½ teaspoon turmeric powder
- Salt and ground black pepper, to taste
- ⅛ teaspoon ground allspice
- Cooking spray

1. Press Start/Cancel. Preheat the air fryer oven to 360ºF (182ºC). Spritz four ramekins with cooking spray.
2. Put equal amounts of each of the ingredients into each ramekin and mix well. Insert the fry basket at mid position.
3. Select Air Fry, Convection, and set time to 16 minutes. ramekins in the fry basket.
4. Serve immediately.

BBQ Pork Steaks

Prep time: 5 minutes | Cook time: 15 minutes | Serves 4

- 4 pork steaks
- 1 tablespoon Cajun seasoning
- 2 tablespoons BBQ sauce
- 1 tablespoon vinegar
- 1 teaspoon soy sauce
- ½ cup brown sugar
- ½ cup ketchup

1. Press Start/Cancel. Preheat the air fryer oven to 290ºF (143ºC).
2. Sprinkle pork steaks with Cajun seasoning.
3. Combine remaining ingredients and brush onto steaks.
4. Add coated steaks to the fry basket. Insert the fry basket at mid position. Select Air Fry, Convection, and set time to 15 minutes, or until just browned.
5. Serve immediately.

Pork Medallions with Radicchio and Endive Salad

Prep time: 25 minutes | Cook time: 7 minutes | Serves 4

- 1 (8-ounce / 227-g) pork tenderloin
- Salt and freshly ground black pepper, to taste
- ¼ cup flour
- 2 eggs, lightly beaten
- ¾ cup cracker meal

Vinaigrette:
- ¼ cup white balsamic vinegar
- 2 tablespoons agave syrup (or honey or maple syrup)
- 1 tablespoon Dijon mustard
- juice of ½ lemon
- 2 tablespoons chopped chervil or flat-leaf parsley
- salt and freshly ground black pepper
- ½ cup extra-virgin olive oil
- Radicchio and Endive Salad:

- 1 teaspoon paprika
- 1 teaspoon dry mustard
- 1 teaspoon garlic powder
- 1 teaspoon dried thyme
- 1 teaspoon salt
- vegetable or canola oil, in spray bottle

- 1 heart romaine lettuce, torn into large pieces
- ½ head radicchio, coarsely chopped
- 2 heads endive, sliced
- ½ cup cherry tomatoes, halved
- 3 ounces (85 g) fresh Mozzarella, diced
- Salt and freshly ground black pepper, to taste

1. Slice the pork tenderloin into 1-inch slices. Using a meat pounder, pound the pork slices into thin ½-inch medallions. Generously season the pork with salt and freshly ground black pepper on both sides.
2. Set up a dredging station using three shallow dishes. Put the flour in one dish and the beaten eggs in a second dish. Combine the cracker meal, paprika, dry mustard, garlic powder, thyme and salt in a third dish.
3. Press Start/Cancel. Preheat the air fryer oven to 400ºF (204ºC).
4. Dredge the pork medallions in flour first and then into the beaten egg. Let the excess egg drip off and coat both sides of the medallions with the cracker meal crumb mixture. Spray both sides of the coated medallions with vegetable or canola oil. Transfer to the fry basket.
5. Insert the fry basket at mid position. Select Air Fry, Convection, and set time to 5 minutes. You may need to work in batches.
6. Once you have air-fried all the medallions, flip them all over and return the first batch of medallions back into the air fryer oven on top of the second batch. Air fry for an additional 2 minutes.
7. While the medallions are cooking, make the salad and dressing. Whisk the white balsamic vinegar, agave syrup, Dijon mustard, lemon juice, chervil, salt and pepper together in a small bowl. Whisk in the olive oil slowly until combined and thickened.
8. Combine the romaine lettuce, radicchio, endive, cherry tomatoes, and Mozzarella cheese in a large salad bowl. Drizzle the dressing over the vegetables and toss to combine. Season with salt and freshly ground black pepper.
9. Serve the pork medallions warm on or beside the salad.

Beef Chuck with Brussels Sprouts

Prep time: 20 minutes | Cook time: 15 minutes | Serves 4

- 1 pound (454 g) beef chuck shoulder steak
- 2 tablespoons vegetable oil
- 1 tablespoon red wine vinegar
- 1 teaspoon fine sea salt
- ½ teaspoon ground black pepper
- 1 teaspoon smoked paprika
- 1 teaspoon onion powder
- ½ teaspoon garlic powder
- ½ pound (227 g) Brussels sprouts, cleaned and halved
- ½ teaspoon fennel seeds
- 1 teaspoon dried basil
- 1 teaspoon dried sage

1. Massage the beef with the vegetable oil, wine vinegar, salt, black pepper, paprika, onion powder, and garlic powder, coating it well.
2. Allow to marinate for a minimum of 3 hours.
3. Press Start/Cancel. Preheat the air fryer oven to 390ºF (199ºC).

4. Remove the beef from the marinade and put in the fry basket. Insert the fry basket at mid position. Select Air Fry, Convection, and set time to 10 minutes. Flip the beef halfway through.
5. Put the prepared Brussels sprouts in the air fryer oven along with the fennel seeds, basil, and sage.
6. Lower the heat to 380ºF (193ºC) and air fry everything for another 5 minutes.
7. Give them a good stir. Air fry for an additional 10 minutes.
8. Serve immediately.

Sun-dried Tomato Crusted Chops

Prep time: 15 minutes | Cook time: 10 minutes | Serves 4

- ½ cup oil-packed sun-dried tomatoes
- ½ cup toasted almonds
- ¼ cup grated Parmesan cheese
- ½ cup olive oil, plus more for brushing the fry basket
- 2 tablespoons water
- ½ teaspoon salt
- Freshly ground black pepper, to taste
- 4 center-cut boneless pork chops (about 1¼ pounds / 567 g)

1. Put the sun-dried tomatoes into a food processor and pulse them until they are coarsely chopped. Add the almonds, Parmesan cheese, olive oil, water, salt and pepper. Process into a smooth paste. Spread most of the paste (leave a little in reserve) onto both sides of the pork chops and then pierce the meat several times with a needle-style meat tenderizer or a fork. Let the pork chops sit and marinate for at least 1 hour (refrigerate if marinating for longer than 1 hour).
2. Press Start/Cancel. Preheat the air fryer oven to 370ºF (188ºC).
3. Brush more olive oil on the bottom of the fry basket. Transfer the pork chops into the fry basket, spooning a little more of the sun-dried tomato paste onto the pork chops if there are any gaps where the paste may have been rubbed off.
4. Insert the fry basket at mid position. Select Air Fry, Convection, and set time to 10 minutes, turning the chops over halfway through.
5. When the pork chops have finished cooking, transfer them to a serving plate and serve.

Bacon and Pear Stuffed Pork Chops

Prep time: 20 minutes | Cook time: 24 minutes | Serves 3

- 4 slices bacon, chopped
- 1 tablespoon butter
- ½ cup finely diced onion
- ⅓ cup chicken stock
- 1½ cups seasoned stuffing cubes
- 1 egg, beaten
- ½ teaspoon dried thyme
- ½ teaspoon salt
- ⅛ teaspoon freshly ground black pepper
- 1 pear, finely diced
- ⅓ cup crumbled blue cheese
- 3 boneless center-cut pork chops (2-inch thick)
- Olive oil, for greasing
- Salt and freshly ground black pepper, to taste

1. Press Start/Cancel. Preheat the air fryer oven to 400ºF (204ºC).
2. Put the bacon into the fry basket and insert the fry basket at mid position. Select Air Fry, Convection, and set time to 6 minutes, stirring halfway through the cooking time. Remove the bacon and set it aside on a paper towel. Pour out the grease from the bottom of the air fryer oven.
3. To make the stuffing, melt the butter in a medium saucepan over medium heat on the stovetop. Add the onion and sauté for a few minutes until it starts to soften. Add the chicken stock and simmer for 1 minute. Remove the pan from the heat and add the stuffing cubes. Stir until the stock has been absorbed. Add the egg, dried thyme, salt and freshly ground black pepper, and stir until combined. Fold in the diced pear and crumbled blue cheese.
4. Put the pork chops on a cutting board. Using the palm of the hand to hold the chop flat and steady, slice into the side of the pork chop to make a pocket in the center of the chop. Leave about an inch of chop uncut and make sure you don't cut all the way through the pork chop. Brush both sides of the pork chops with olive oil and season with salt and freshly ground black pepper. Stuff each pork chop with a third of the stuffing, packing the stuffing tightly inside the pocket.
5. Press Start/Cancel. Preheat the air fryer oven to 360ºF (182ºC).
6. Spray or brush the sides of the fry basket with oil. Put the pork chops in the fry basket with the open, stuffed edge of the pork chop facing the outside edges of the basket.
7. Insert the fry basket at mid position. Select Air Fry, Convection, and set time to 18 minutes, turning the pork chops over halfway through the cooking time. When the chops are done, let them rest for 5 minutes and then transfer to a serving platter.

Spinach and Beef Braciole

Prep time: 25 minutes | Cook time: 1 hour 32 minutes | Serves 4

- ½ onion, finely chopped
- 1 teaspoon olive oil
- ⅓ cup red wine
- 2 cups crushed tomatoes
- 1 teaspoon Italian seasoning
- ½ teaspoon garlic powder
- ¼ teaspoon crushed red pepper flakes
- 2 tablespoons chopped fresh parsley
- 2 top round steaks (about 1½ pounds / 680 g)
- salt and freshly ground black pepper
- 2 cups fresh spinach, chopped
- 1 clove minced garlic
- ½ cup roasted red peppers, julienned
- ½ cup grated pecorino cheese
- ¼ cup pine nuts, toasted and roughly chopped
- 2 tablespoons olive oil

1. Press Start/Cancel. Preheat the air fryer oven to 400ºF (204ºC).
2. Toss the onions and olive oil together in a baking pan or casserole dish. Insert at mid position. Select Air Fry, Convection, and set time to 5 minutes, stirring a couple times during the cooking process. Add the red wine, crushed tomatoes, Italian seasoning, garlic powder, red pepper flakes and parsley and stir. Cover the pan tightly with aluminum foil, lower the air fryer oven temperature to 350ºF (177ºC) and continue to air fry for 15 minutes.
3. While the sauce is simmering, prepare the beef. Using a meat mallet, pound the beef until it is ¼-inch thick. Season both sides of the beef with salt and pepper. Combine the spinach, garlic, red peppers, pecorino cheese, pine nuts and olive oil in a medium bowl. Season with salt and freshly ground black pepper. Disperse the mixture over the steaks. Starting at one of the short ends, roll the beef around the filling, tucking in the sides as you roll to ensure the filling is completely enclosed. Secure the beef rolls with toothpicks.
4. Remove the baking pan with the sauce from the air fryer oven and set it aside. Press Start/Cancel. Preheat the air fryer oven to 400ºF (204ºC).
5. Brush or spray the beef rolls with a little olive oil and air fry for 12 minutes, rotating the beef during the cooking process for even browning. When the beef is browned, submerge the rolls into the sauce in the baking pan, cover the pan with foil and return it to the air fryer oven. Reduce the temperature of the air fryer oven to 250ºF (121ºC) and air fry for 60 minutes.
6. Remove the beef rolls from the sauce. Cut each roll into slices and serve, ladling some sauce over top.

CHAPTER 9

FISH AND SEAFOOD

67	Roasted Salmon Fillets
67	Crispy Coconut Shrimp
68	Crab Cakes with Sriracha Mayonnaise
69	Orange-Mustard Glazed Salmon
69	Thai Shrimp Skewers with Peanut Dipping Sauce
70	Cornmeal-Crusted Trout Fingers
71	Sole and Asparagus Bundles
72	Roasted Cod with Lemon-Garlic Potatoes
73	Moroccan Spiced Halibut with Chickpea Salad
74	Swordfish Skewers with Caponata
75	Crunchy Air Fried Cod Fillets

Roasted Salmon Fillets

Prep time: 5 minutes | Cook time: 12 minutes | Serves 2

- 2 (8-ounce / 227 -g) skin-on salmon fillets, 1½ inches thick
- 1 teaspoon vegetable oil
- Salt and pepper, to taste
- Vegetable oil spray

1. Press Start/Cancel. Preheat the air fryer oven to 400ºF (204ºC).
2. Make foil sling for fry basket by folding 1 long sheet of aluminum foil so it is 4 inches wide. Lay sheet of foil widthwise across basket, pressing foil into and up sides of basket. Fold excess foil as needed so that edges of foil are flush with top of basket. Lightly spray foil and basket with vegetable oil spray.
3. Pat salmon dry with paper towels, rub with oil, and season with salt and pepper. Arrange fillets skin side down on sling in prepared basket, spaced evenly apart. Insert the fry basket at mid position.
4. Select Air Fry, Convection, and set time to 12 minutes, or until center is still translucent when checked with the tip of a paring knife and registers 125ºF (52ºC) (for medium-rare), using sling to rotate fillets halfway through cooking.
5. Using the sling, carefully remove salmon from air fryer oven. Slide fish spatula along underside of fillets and transfer to individual serving plates, leaving skin behind. Serve.

Crispy Coconut Shrimp

Prep time: 15 minutes | Cook time: 8 minutes | Serves 4

Sweet Chili Mayo:
- 3 tablespoons mayonnaise
- 3 tablespoons Thai sweet chili sauce
- 1 tablespoon Sriracha sauce

Shrimp:
- ⅔ cup sweetened shredded coconut
- ⅔ cup panko bread crumbs
- Kosher salt, to taste
- 2 tablespoons all-purpose or gluten-free flour
- 2 large eggs
- 24 extra-jumbo shrimp (about 1 pound / 454 g), peeled and deveined
- Cooking spray

1. In a medium bowl, combine the mayonnaise, Thai sweet chili sauce, and Sriracha and mix well.
2. In a medium bowl, combine the coconut, panko, and ¼ teaspoon salt. Place the flour in a shallow bowl. Whisk the eggs in another shallow bowl.

3. Season the shrimp with ⅛ teaspoon salt. Dip the shrimp in the flour, shaking off any excess, then into the egg. Coat in the coconut-panko mixture, gently pressing to adhere, then transfer to a large plate. Spray both sides of the shrimp with oil.
4. Press Start/Cancel. Preheat the air fryer oven to 360ºF (182ºC).
5. Working in batches, arrange a single layer of the shrimp in the fry basket. Insert the fry basket at mid position. Select Air Fry, Convection, and set time to 8 minutes, flipping halfway, until the crust is golden brown and the shrimp are cooked through.
6. Serve with the sweet chili mayo for dipping.

Crab Cakes with Sriracha Mayonnaise

Prep time: 15 minutes | Cook time: 10 minutes | Serves 4

Sriracha Mayonnaise:
- 1 cup mayonnaise
- 1 tablespoon sriracha
- 1½ teaspoons freshly squeezed lemon juice

Crab Cakes:
- 1 teaspoon extra-virgin olive oil
- ¼ cup finely diced red bell pepper
- ¼ cup diced onion
- ¼ cup diced celery
- 1 pound (454 g) lump crab meat
- 1 teaspoon Old Bay seasoning
- 1 egg
- 1½ teaspoons freshly squeezed lemon juice
- 1¾ cups panko bread crumbs, divided
- Vegetable oil, for spraying

1. Mix the mayonnaise, sriracha, and lemon juice in a small bowl. Place ⅔ cup of the mixture in a separate bowl to form the base of the crab cakes. Cover the remaining sriracha mayonnaise and refrigerate. (This will become dipping sauce for the crab cakes once they are cooked.)
2. Heat the olive oil in a heavy-bottomed, medium skillet over medium-high heat. Add the bell pepper, onion, and celery and sauté for 3 minutes. Transfer the vegetables to the bowl with the reserved ⅔ cup of sriracha mayonnaise. Mix in the crab, Old Bay seasoning, egg, and lemon juice. Add 1 cup of the panko. Form the crab mixture into 8 cakes. Dredge the cakes in the remaining ¾ cup of panko, turning to coat. Place on a baking sheet. Cover and refrigerate for at least 1 hour and up to 8 hours.
3. Press Start/Cancel. Preheat the air fryer oven to 375ºF (191ºC). Spray the fry basket with oil. Working in batches as needed so as not to overcrowd the basket, place the chilled crab cakes in a single layer in the basket. Spray the crab cakes with oil. Insert the basket at low position.
4. Select Bake, Convection, and set time to 9 minutes, or until golden brown, carefully turning halfway through cooking. Remove to a platter and keep warm. Repeat with the remaining crab cakes as needed.
5. Serve the crab cakes immediately with sriracha mayonnaise dipping sauce.

Orange-Mustard Glazed Salmon

Prep time: 10 minutes | Cook time: 12 minutes | Serves 2

- 1 tablespoon orange marmalade
- ¼ teaspoon grated orange zest plus 1 tablespoon juice
- 2 teaspoons whole-grain mustard
- 2 (8-ounce / 227 -g) skin-on salmon fillets, 1½ inches thick
- Salt and pepper, to taste
- Vegetable oil spray

1. Press Start/Cancel. Preheat the air fryer oven to 400ºF (204ºC).
2. Make foil sling for fry basket by folding 1 long sheet of aluminum foil so it is 4 inches wide. Lay sheet of foil widthwise across basket, pressing foil into and up sides of basket. Fold excess foil as needed so that edges of foil are flush with top of basket. Lightly spray foil and basket with vegetable oil spray.
3. Combine marmalade, orange zest and juice, and mustard in bowl. Pat salmon dry with paper towels and season with salt and pepper. Brush tops and sides of fillets evenly with glaze. Arrange fillets skin side down on sling in prepared basket, spaced evenly apart. Insert the fry basket at mid position.
4. Select Air Fry, Convection, and set time to 12 minutes, or until center is still translucent when checked with the tip of a paring knife and registers 125ºF (52ºC) (for medium-rare), using sling to rotate fillets halfway through cooking.
5. Using the sling, carefully remove salmon from air fryer oven. Slide fish spatula along underside of fillets and transfer to individual serving plates, leaving skin behind. Serve.

Thai Shrimp Skewers with Peanut Dipping Sauce

Prep time: 15 minutes | Cook time: 7 minutes | Serves 2

- Salt and pepper, to taste
- 12 ounces (340 g) extra-large shrimp, peeled and deveined
- 1 tablespoon vegetable oil
- 1 teaspoon honey
- ½ teaspoon grated lime zest plus 1 tablespoon juice, plus lime wedges for serving
- 6 (6-inch) wooden skewers
- 3 tablespoons creamy peanut butter
- 3 tablespoons hot tap water
- 1 tablespoon chopped fresh cilantro
- 1 teaspoon fish sauce

1. Press Start/Cancel. Preheat the air fryer oven to 400ºF (204ºC).

2. Dissolve 2 tablespoons salt in 1 quart cold water in a large container. Add shrimp, cover, and refrigerate for 15 minutes.
3. Remove shrimp from brine and pat dry with paper towels. Whisk oil, honey, lime zest, and ¼ teaspoon pepper together in a large bowl. Add shrimp and toss to coat. Thread shrimp onto skewers, leaving about ¼ inch between each shrimp (3 or 4 shrimp per skewer).
4. Arrange 3 skewers in fry basket, parallel to each other and spaced evenly apart. Arrange remaining 3 skewers on top, perpendicular to the bottom layer. Insert the fry basket at mid position.
5. Select Air Fry, Convection, and set time to 7 minutes, or until shrimp are opaque throughout, flipping and rotating skewers halfway through cooking.
6. Whisk peanut butter, hot tap water, lime juice, cilantro, and fish sauce together in a bowl until smooth. Serve skewers with peanut dipping sauce and lime wedges.

Cornmeal-Crusted Trout Fingers

Prep time: 15 minutes | Cook time: 6 minutes | Serves 2

- ½ cup yellow cornmeal, medium or finely ground (not coarse)
- ⅓ cup all-purpose flour
- 1½ teaspoons baking powder
- 1 teaspoon kosher salt, plus more as needed
- ½ teaspoon freshly ground black pepper, plus more as needed
- ⅛ teaspoon cayenne pepper
- ¾ pound (340 g) skinless trout fillets, cut into strips 1 inch wide and 3 inches long
- 3 large eggs, lightly beaten
- Cooking spray
- ½ cup mayonnaise
- 2 tablespoons capers, rinsed and finely chopped
- 1 tablespoon fresh tarragon
- 1 teaspoon fresh lemon juice, plus lemon wedges, for serving

1. Press Start/Cancel. Preheat the air fryer oven to 400ºF (204ºC).
2. In a large bowl, whisk together the cornmeal, flour, baking powder, salt, black pepper, and cayenne. Dip the trout strips in the egg, then toss them in the cornmeal mixture until fully coated. Transfer the trout to a rack set over a baking sheet and liberally spray all over with cooking spray.
3. Transfer half the fish to the air fryer oven and insert at mid position. Select Air Fry, Convection, and set time to 6 minutes, or until the fish is cooked through and golden brown. Transfer the fish sticks to a plate and repeat with the remaining fish.
4. Meanwhile, in a bowl, whisk together the mayonnaise, capers, tarragon, and lemon juice. Season the tartar sauce with salt and black pepper.
5. Serve the trout fingers hot along with the tartar sauce and lemon wedges.

Sole and Asparagus Bundles

Prep time: 10 minutes | Cook time: 19 minutes | Serves 2

- 8 ounces (227 g) asparagus, trimmed
- 1 teaspoon extra-virgin olive oil, divided
- Salt and pepper, to taste
- 4 (3-ounce / 85-g) skinless sole or flounder fillets, ⅛ to ¼ inch thick
- 4 tablespoons unsalted butter, softened
- 1 small shallot, minced
- 1 tablespoon chopped fresh tarragon
- ¼ teaspoon lemon zest plus ½ teaspoon juice
- Vegetable oil spray

1. Press Start/Cancel. Preheat the air fryer oven to 300ºF (149ºC).
2. Toss asparagus with ½ teaspoon oil, pinch salt, and pinch pepper in a bowl. Cover and microwave until bright green and just tender, about 3 minutes, tossing halfway through microwaving. Uncover and set aside to cool slightly.
3. Make foil sling for fry basket by folding 1 long sheet of aluminum foil so it is 4 inches wide. Lay sheet of foil widthwise across basket, pressing foil into and up sides of basket. Fold excess foil as needed so that edges of foil are flush with top of basket. Lightly spray foil and basket with vegetable oil spray.
4. Pat sole dry with paper towels and season with salt and pepper. Arrange fillets skinned side up on cutting board, with thicker ends closest to you. Arrange asparagus evenly across base of each fillet, then tightly roll fillets away from you around asparagus to form tidy bundles.
5. Rub bundles evenly with remaining ½ teaspoon oil and arrange seam side down on sling in prepared basket. Insert at low position.
6. Select Bake, Convection, and set time to 16 minutes, or until asparagus is tender and sole flakes apart when gently prodded with a paring knife, using a sling to rotate bundles halfway through cooking.
7. Combine butter, shallot, tarragon, and lemon zest and juice in a bowl. Using sling, carefully remove sole bundles from air fryer oven and transfer to individual plates. Top evenly with butter mixture and serve.

Roasted Cod with Lemon-Garlic Potatoes

Prep time: 10 minutes | Cook time: 30 minutes | Serves 2

- 3 tablespoons unsalted butter, softened, divided
- 2 garlic cloves, minced
- 1 lemon, grated to yield 2 teaspoons zest and sliced ¼ inch thick
- Salt and pepper, to taste
- 1 large russet potato (12 ounce / 340-g), unpeeled, sliced ¼ inch thick
- 1 tablespoon minced fresh parsley, chives, or tarragon
- 2 (8-ounce / 227-g) skinless cod fillets, 1¼ inches thick
- Vegetable oil spray

1. Press Start/Cancel. Preheat the air fryer oven to 400ºF (204ºC).
2. Make foil sling for fry basket by folding 1 long sheet of aluminum foil so it is 4 inches wide. Lay sheet of foil widthwise across basket, pressing foil into and up sides of basket. Fold excess foil as needed so that edges of foil are flush with top of basket. Lightly spray the foil and basket with vegetable oil spray.
3. Microwave 1 tablespoon butter, garlic, 1 teaspoon lemon zest, ¼ teaspoon salt, and ⅛ teaspoon pepper in a medium bowl, stirring once, until the butter is melted and the mixture is fragrant, about 30 seconds. Add the potato slices and toss to coat. Shingle the potato slices on sling in prepared basket to create 2 even layers. Insert the fry basket at mid position.
4. Select Air Fry, Convection, and set time to 17 minutes, or until potato slices are spotty brown and just tender, using a sling to rotate potatoes halfway through cooking.
5. Combine the remaining 2 tablespoons butter, remaining 1 teaspoon lemon zest, and parsley in a small bowl. Pat the cod dry with paper towels and season with salt and pepper. Place the fillets, skinned-side down, on top of potato slices, spaced evenly apart. (Tuck thinner tail ends of fillets under themselves as needed to create uniform pieces.) Dot the fillets with the butter mixture and top with the lemon slices. Return the basket to the air fryer oven and air fry until the cod flakes apart when gently prodded with a paring knife and registers 140ºF (60ºC), 13 minutes, using a sling to rotate the potato slices and cod halfway through cooking.
6. Using a sling, carefully remove potatoes and cod from air fryer oven. Cut the potato slices into 2 portions between fillets using fish spatula. Slide spatula along underside of potato slices and transfer with cod to individual plates. Serve.

Moroccan Spiced Halibut with Chickpea Salad

Prep time: 15 minutes | Cook time: 16 minutes | Serves 2

- ¾ teaspoon ground coriander
- ½ teaspoon ground cumin
- ¼ teaspoon ground ginger
- ⅛ teaspoon ground cinnamon
- Salt and pepper, to taste
- 2 (8-ounce / 227-g) skinless halibut fillets, 1¼ inches thick
- 4 teaspoons extra-virgin olive oil, divided, plus extra for drizzling
- 1 (15-ounce / 425-g) can chickpeas, rinsed
- 1 tablespoon lemon juice, plus lemon wedges for serving
- 1 teaspoon harissa
- ½ teaspoon honey
- 2 carrots, peeled and shredded
- 2 tablespoons chopped fresh mint, divided
- Vegetable oil spray

1. Press Start/Cancel. Preheat the air fryer oven to 300ºF (149ºC).
2. Make foil sling for fry basket by folding 1 long sheet of aluminum foil so it is 4 inches wide. Lay sheet of foil widthwise across basket, pressing foil into and up sides of basket. Fold excess foil as needed so that edges of foil are flush with top of basket. Lightly spray foil and basket with vegetable oil spray.
3. Combine coriander, cumin, ginger, cinnamon, ⅛ teaspoon salt, and ⅛ teaspoon pepper in a small bowl. Pat halibut dry with paper towels, rub with 1 teaspoon oil, and sprinkle all over with spice mixture. Arrange fillets, skinned side down, on sling in prepared basket, spaced evenly apart. Insert at low position.
4. Select Bake, Convection, and set time to 14 minutes, or until halibut flakes apart when gently prodded with a paring knife and registers 140ºF (60ºC), using the sling to rotate fillets halfway through cooking.
5. Meanwhile, microwave chickpeas in medium bowl until heated through, about 2 minutes. Stir in remaining 1 tablespoon oil, lemon juice, harissa, honey, ⅛ teaspoon salt, and ⅛ teaspoon pepper. Add carrots and 1 tablespoon mint and toss to combine. Season with salt and pepper, to taste.
6. Using sling, carefully remove halibut from air fryer oven and transfer to individual plates. Sprinkle with remaining 1 tablespoon mint and drizzle with extra oil to taste. Serve with salad and lemon wedges.

Swordfish Skewers with Caponata

Prep time: 15 minutes | Cook time: 21 minutes | Serves 2

- 1 (10-ounce / 283-g) small Italian eggplant, cut into 1-inch pieces
- 6 ounces (170 g) cherry tomatoes
- 3 scallions, cut into 2 inches long
- 2 tablespoons extra-virgin olive oil, divided
- Salt and pepper, to taste
- 12 ounces (340 g) skinless swordfish steaks, 1¼ inches thick, cut into 1-inch pieces
- 2 teaspoons honey, divided
- 2 teaspoons ground coriander, divided
- 1 teaspoon grated lemon zest, divided
- 1 teaspoon juice
- 4 (6-inch) wooden skewers
- 1 garlic clove, minced
- ½ teaspoon ground cumin
- 1 tablespoon chopped fresh basil

1. Press Start/Cancel. Preheat the air fryer oven to 400ºF (204ºC).
2. Toss eggplant, tomatoes, and scallions with 1 tablespoon oil, ¼ teaspoon salt, and ⅛ teaspoon pepper in bowl; transfer to fry basket. Insert the fry basket at mid position. Select Air Fry, Convection, and set time to 14 minutes, or until eggplant is softened and browned and tomatoes have begun to burst, tossing halfway through cooking. Transfer vegetables to cutting board and set aside to cool slightly.
3. Pat swordfish dry with paper towels. Combine 1 teaspoon oil, 1 teaspoon honey, 1 teaspoon coriander, ½ teaspoon lemon zest, ⅛ teaspoon salt, and pinch pepper in a clean bowl. Add swordfish and toss to coat. Thread swordfish onto skewers, leaving about ¼ inch between each piece (3 or 4 pieces per skewer).
4. Arrange skewers in fry basket, spaced evenly apart. (Skewers may overlap slightly.) Return basket to air fryer oven and air fry until swordfish is browned and registers 140ºF (60ºC), 7 minutes, flipping and rotating skewers halfway through cooking.
5. Meanwhile, combine remaining 2 teaspoons oil, remaining 1 teaspoon honey, remaining 1 teaspoon coriander, remaining ½ teaspoon lemon zest, lemon juice, garlic, cumin, ¼ teaspoon salt, and ⅛ teaspoon pepper in large bowl. Microwave, stirring once, until fragrant, about 30 seconds. Coarsely chop the cooked vegetables, transfer to bowl with dressing, along with any accumulated juices, and gently toss to combine. Stir in basil and season with salt and pepper to taste. Serve skewers with caponata.

Crunchy Air Fried Cod Fillets

Prep time: 10 minutes | Cook time: 14 minutes | Serves 2

- 1/3 cup panko bread crumbs
- 1 teaspoon vegetable oil
- 1 small shallot, minced
- 1 small garlic clove, minced
- ½ teaspoon minced fresh thyme
- Salt and pepper, to taste
- 1 tablespoon minced fresh parsley
- 1 tablespoon mayonnaise
- 1 large egg yolk
- ¼ teaspoon grated lemon zest, plus lemon wedges for serving
- 2 (8-ounce / 227-g) skinless cod fillets, 1¼ inches thick
- Vegetable oil spray

1. Press Start/Cancel. Preheat the air fryer oven to 300ºF (149ºC).
2. Make foil sling for fry basket by folding 1 long sheet of aluminum foil so it is 4 inches wide. Lay sheet of foil widthwise across basket, pressing foil into and up sides of basket. Fold excess foil as needed so that edges of foil are flush with top of basket. Lightly spray the foil and basket with vegetable oil spray.
3. Toss the panko with the oil in a bowl until evenly coated. Stir in the shallot, garlic, thyme, ¼ teaspoon salt, and ⅛ teaspoon pepper. Microwave, stirring frequently, until the panko is light golden brown, about 2 minutes. Transfer to a shallow dish and let cool slightly; stir in the parsley. Whisk the mayonnaise, egg yolk, lemon zest, and ⅛ teaspoon pepper together in another bowl.
4. Pat the cod dry with paper towels and season with salt and pepper. Arrange the fillets, skinned-side down, on plate and brush tops evenly with mayonnaise mixture. (Tuck thinner tail ends of fillets under themselves as needed to create uniform pieces.) Working with 1 fillet at a time, dredge the coated side in panko mixture, pressing gently to adhere. Arrange the fillets, crumb-side up, on sling in the prepared basket, spaced evenly apart. Insert at low position.
5. Select Bake, Convection, and set time to 14 minutes, using a sling to rotate fillets halfway through cooking. Using a sling, carefully remove cod from air fryer oven. Serve with the lemon wedges.

CHAPTER 10

ROTISSERIE RECIPES

78 Honey Glazed Rotisserie Ham
78 Rotisserie Chicken with Lemon
79 Air Fried Beef Roast
80 Apple and Carrot Stuffed Rotisserie Turkey
80 Sriracha Honey Pork Tenderloin
81 Marinated Medium Rare Rotisserie Beef
82 Red Wine Rotisserie Lamb Leg
83 Bourbon Rotisserie Pork Shoulder
84 Greek Rotisserie Lamb Leg
85 Whole Rotisserie Chicken

Honey Glazed Rotisserie Ham

Prep time: 20 minutes | Cook time: 3 hours | Serves 6

- 1 (5-pound/2.3-kg) cooked boneless ham, pat dry

For the Glaze:
- ½ cup honey
- 2 teaspoons lemon juice
- 1 teaspoon ground cloves
- 1 teaspoon cinnamon
- ½ cup brown sugar

1. Using the rotisserie shaft, push through the ham and attach the rotisserie forks.
2. If desired, place aluminum foil onto the drip pan. (It makes for easier clean-up!)
3. Set the oven to Roast, set temperature to 250°F (121°C), Rotate, and set time to 3 hours. Press Start to begin preheating.
4. Once preheated, place the prepared ham with rotisserie shaft into the oven.
5. Meanwhile, combine the ingredients for the glaze in a small bowl. Stir to mix well.
6. When the ham has reached 145°F (63°C), brush the glaze mixture over all surfaces of the ham.
7. When cooking is complete, remove the ham using the rotisserie handle and, using hot pads or gloves, carefully remove the ham from the shaft.
8. Let it rest for 10 minutes covered loosely with foil and then carve and serve.

Rotisserie Chicken with Lemon

Prep time: 10 minutes | Cook time: 40 minutes | Serves 6

- 1 (4 pounds / 1.8 kg) whole chicken
- 2 teaspoons paprika
- 1½ teaspoons thyme
- 1 teaspoon onion powder
- 1 teaspoon garlic powder
- Salt and pepper, to taste
- ¼ cup butter, melted
- 2 tablespoons olive oil
- 1 lemon, sliced
- 2 sprigs rosemary

1. Remove the giblets from the chicken cavity and carefully loosen the skin starting at the neck.
2. In a bowl, mix together the paprika, thyme, onion powder, garlic powder, salt, and pepper. Set aside.

3. Rub the melted butter under the skin and pat the skin back into place.
4. Truss the chicken, ensuring the wings and legs are tied closely together and the cavity is closed up.
5. Drizzle the olive oil all over the chicken and rub it into the chicken.
6. Rub the spice mixture onto the chicken's skin.
7. Place the lemon slices and sprigs of rosemary into the cavity.
8. Using the rotisserie shaft, push through the chicken and attach the rotisserie forks.
9. If desired, place aluminum foil onto the drip pan. (It makes for easier clean-up!)
10. Select Roast, Super Convection, set the temperature to 380ºF (193ºC), Rotate, and set the time for 40 minutes. Select Start to begin preheating.
11. Once the unit has preheated, place the prepared chicken with the rotisserie shaft into the oven.
12. When cooking is complete, remove the chicken using the rotisserie handle and, using hot pads or gloves, carefully remove the chicken from the shaft.
13. Let sit for 10 minutes before slicing and serving.

Air Fried Beef Roast

Prep time: 5 minutes | Cook time: 38 minutes | Serves 6

- 2.5 pound (1.1 kg) beef roast
- 1 tablespoon olive oil
- 1 tablespoon Poultry seasoning

1. Tie the beef roast and rub the olive oil all over the roast. Sprinkle with the seasoning.
2. Using the rotisserie shaft, push through the beef roast and attach the rotisserie forks.
3. If desired, place aluminum foil onto the drip pan. (It makes for easier clean-up!)
4. Select Air Fry, Super Convection. Set temperature to 360ºF (182ºC), Rotate, and set time to 38 minutes for medium rare beef. Select Start to begin preheating.
5. When the unit has preheated, place the prepared chicken with rotisserie shaft into the oven.
6. When cooking is complete, remove the beef roast using the rotisserie handle and, using hot pads or gloves, carefully remove the beef roast from the shaft.
7. Let cool for 5 minutes before serving.

Apple and Carrot Stuffed Rotisserie Turkey

Prep time: 30 minutes | Cook time: 3 hours | Serves 12 to 14

- 1 (12-pound/5.4-kg) turkey, giblet removed, rinsed and pat dry

For the Seasoning:
- ¼ cup lemon pepper
- 2 tablespoons chopped fresh parsley
- 1 tablespoon celery salt
- 2 cloves garlic, minced
- 2 teaspoons ground black pepper
- 1 teaspoon sage

For the Stuffing:
- 1 medium onion, cut into 8 equal parts
- 1 carrot, sliced
- 1 apple, cored and cut into 8 thick slices

1. Mix together the seasoning in a small bowl. Rub over the surface and inside of the turkey.
2. Stuff the turkey with the onions, carrots, and apples. Using the rotisserie shaft, push through the turkey and attach the rotisserie forks.
3. If desired, place aluminum foil onto the drip pan. (It makes for easier clean-up!)
4. Set the oven to Roast, set temperature to 350ºF (180ºC), Rotate, and set time to 3 hours. Press Start to begin preheating.
5. Once preheated, place the prepared turkey with rotisserie shaft into the oven.
6. When cooking is complete, the internal temperature should read at least 180ºF (82ºC). Remove the lamb leg using the rotisserie handle and, using hot pads or gloves, carefully remove the turkey from the shaft.
7. Server hot.

Sriracha Honey Pork Tenderloin

Prep time: 20 minutes | Cook time: 25 minutes | Serves 2 to 3

- 1 pound (454 g) pork tenderloin
- 2 tablespoons Sriracha hot sauce
- 2 tablespoons honey
- 1½ teaspoons kosher salt

1. Stir together the Sriracha hot sauce, honey and salt in a bowl. Rub the sauce all over the pork tenderloin.
2. Using the rotisserie shaft, push through the pork tenderloin and attach the rotisserie forks.

3. If desired, place aluminum foil onto the drip pan. (It makes for easier clean-up!)
4. Select Air Fry, Super Convection, set temperature to 350ºF (180ºC), Rotate, and set time to 20 minutes. Select Start to begin preheating.
5. Once preheated, place the prepared pork tenderloin with rotisserie shaft into the oven.
6. When cooking is complete, remove the pork tenderloin using the rotisserie handle and, using hot pads or gloves, carefully remove the chicken from the shaft.
7. Let rest for 5 minutes and serve.

Marinated Medium Rare Rotisserie Beef

Prep time: 15 minutes | Cook time: 1 hour 40 minutes | Serves 6 to 8

- 5 pounds (2.3 kg) eye round beef roast
- 2 onions, sliced
- 3 cups white wine
- 3 cloves garlic, minced
- 1 teaspoon chopped fresh rosemary
- 1 teaspoon celery seeds
- 1 teaspoon fresh thyme leaves
- ¾ cup olive oil
- 1 tablespoon coarse sea salt
- 1 tablespoon ground black pepper
- 1 teaspoon dried sage
- 2 tablespoons unsalted butter

1. Place beef roast and onions in a large resealable bag.
2. In a small bowl, combine the wine, garlic, rosemary, celery seeds, thyme leaves, oil, salt, pepper, and sage.
3. Pour the marinade mixture over the beef roast and seal the bag. Refrigerate the roast for up to one day.
4. Remove the beef roast from the marinade. Using the rotisserie shaft, push through the beef roast and attach the rotisserie forks.
5. If desired, place aluminum foil onto the drip pan. (It makes for easier clean-up!)
6. Set the oven to Roast, set temperature to 400ºF (205ºC), Rotate, and set time to 1 hour 40 minutes. Press Start to begin preheating.
7. Once preheated, place the prepared lamb leg with rotisserie shaft into the oven. Baste the beef roast with marinade for every 30 minutes.
8. When cooking is complete, remove the lamb leg using the rotisserie handle and, using hot pads or gloves, carefully remove the lamb leg from the shaft.
9. Remove the roast to a platter and allow the roast to rest for 10 minutes.
10. Slice thin and serve.

Red Wine Rotisserie Lamb Leg

Prep time: 25 minutes | Cook time: 1 hour 30 hours | Serves 6 to 8

1 (5-pound / 2.3-kg) leg of lamb, bone-in, fat trimmed, rinsed and drained

For the Marinade:
- ¼ cup dry red wine
- 1 large shallot, roughly chopped
- 4 garlic cloves, peeled and roughly chopped
- 5 large sage leaves
- Juice of 1 lemon
- 2 teaspoons Worcestershire sauce
- ½ teaspoon allspice
- ¾ cup fresh mint leaves
- 3 tablespoons fresh rosemary
- ⅓ cup beef stock
- ½ teaspoon coriander powder
- 2 teaspoons brown sugar
- ½ teaspoon cayenne pepper
- ½ cup olive oil
- 2 teaspoons salt
- 1 teaspoon black pepper

For the Baste:
- 1 cup beef stock
- ¼ cup marinade mixture
- Garnish: salt and black pepper

1. Combine the marinade ingredients in a large bowl. Stir to mix well. Remove ¼ cup of the marinade and set aside.
2. Apply remaining marinade onto lamb leg. Place the lamb leg into a baking dish, cover and refrigerate for 1 to 2 hours.
3. Combine the ingredients for the baste in a small bowl. Stir to mix well. Set aside until ready to use.
4. Using the rotisserie shaft, push through the lamb leg and attach the rotisserie forks.
5. If desired, place aluminum foil onto the drip pan. (It makes for easier clean-up!)
6. Set the oven to Roast, set temperature to 350ºF (180ºC), Rotate, and set time to 1 hour 30 minutes. Press Start to begin preheating.
7. Once preheated, place the prepared lamb leg with rotisserie shaft into the oven.
8. After the first 30 minutes of cooking, apply the baste over the lamb leg for every 20 minutes.
9. When cooking is complete, remove the lamb leg using the rotisserie handle and, using hot pads or gloves, carefully remove the lamb leg from the shaft.
10. Carve and serve.

Bourbon Rotisserie Pork Shoulder

Prep time: 30 minutes | Cook time: 4 hours 30 minutes | Serves 6 to 8

- 1 (5-pound / 2.3-kg) boneless pork shoulder

For the Rub:
- 2 teaspoons ground black peppercorns
- 2 teaspoons ground mustard seed
- 2 tablespoons light brown sugar

For the Mop:
- 1 cup bourbon
- 1 small onion, granulated
- ¼ cup corn syrup
- 1 tablespoon kosher salt
- 1 teaspoon onion powder
- 1 teaspoon garlic powder
- 1 teaspoon paprika
- ¼ cup ketchup
- 2 tablespoons brown mustard
- ½ cup light brown sugar

1. Combine the ingredients for the rub in a small bowl. Stir to mix well.
2. Season pork shoulder all over with rub, wrap in plastic, and place in refrigerator for 12 to 15 hours.
3. Remove roast from the fridge and let meat stand at room temperature for 30 to 45 minutes. Season with kosher salt.
4. Whisk ingredients for mop in a medium bowl. Set aside until ready to use.
5. Using the rotisserie shaft, push through the pork should and attach the rotisserie forks.
6. If desired, place aluminum foil onto the drip pan. (It makes for easier clean-up!)
7. Set the oven to Roast, set temperature to 450ºF (235ºC), Rotate, and set time to 30 minutes. Press Start to begin preheating.
8. Once preheated, place the prepared pork with rotisserie shaft into the oven.
9. After 30 minutes, reduce the temperature to 250ºF (121ºC) and roast for 4 more hours or until an meat thermometer inserted in the center of the pork reads at least 145ºF (63ºC).
10. After the first hour of cooking, apply mop over the pork for every 20 minutes.
11. When cooking is complete, remove the pork using the rotisserie handle and, using hot pads or gloves, carefully remove the pork tenderloin from the shaft.
12. Let stand for 10 minutes before slicing and serving.

Greek Rotisserie Lamb Leg

Prep time: 25 minutes | Cook time: 1 hour 30 minutes | Serves 4 to 6

- 3 pounds (1.4 kg) leg of lamb, boned in

For the Marinade:
- 1 tablespoon lemon zest (about 1 lemon)
- 3 tablespoons lemon juice (about 1½ lemons)
- 3 cloves garlic, minced
- 1 teaspoon onion powder
- 1 teaspoon fresh thyme
- ¼ cup fresh oregano
- ¼ cup olive oil
- 1 teaspoon ground black pepper

For the Herb Dressing:
- 1 tablespoon lemon juice (about ½ lemon)
- ¼ cup chopped fresh oregano
- 1 teaspoon fresh thyme
- 1 tablespoon olive oil
- 1 teaspoon sea salt
- Ground black pepper, to taste

1. Place lamb leg into a large resealable plastic bag. Combine the ingredients for the marinade in a small bowl. Stir to mix well.
2. Pour the marinade over the lamb, making sure the meat is completely coated. Seal the bag and place in the refrigerator. Marinate for 4 to 6 hours before grilling.
3. Remove the lamb leg from the marinade. Using the rotisserie shaft, push through the lamb leg and attach the rotisserie forks.
4. If desired, place aluminum foil onto the drip pan. (It makes for easier clean-up!)
5. Set the oven to Roast, set temperature to 350ºF (180ºC), Rotate, and set time to 1 hour 30 minutes. Press Start to begin preheating.
6. Once preheated, place the prepared lamb leg with rotisserie shaft into the oven. Baste with marinade for every 30 minutes.
7. Meanwhile, combine the ingredients for the herb dressing in a bowl. Stir to mix well.
8. When cooking is complete, remove the lamb leg using the rotisserie handle and, using hot pads or gloves, carefully remove the lamb leg from the shaft.
9. Cover lightly with aluminum foil for 8 to 10 minutes.
10. Carve the leg and arrange on a platter,. Drizzle with herb dressing. Serve immediately.

Whole Rotisserie Chicken

Prep time: 10 minutes | Cook time: 45 minutes | Serves 4

- 3 pounds (1.4 kg) tied whole chicken
- 3 cloves garlic, halved

Chicken Rub:
- ½ teaspoon fresh ground pepper
- ½ teaspoon salt
- 1 teaspoon garlic powder
- 1 whole lemon, quartered
- 2 sprigs fresh rosemary whole
- 2 tablespoons olive oil

- 1 teaspoon dried oregano
- 1 teaspoon paprika
- 1 sprig rosemary (leaves only)

1. Mix together the rub ingredients in a small bowl. Set aside.
2. Place the chicken on a clean cutting board. Ensure the cavity of the chicken is clean. Stuff the chicken cavity with the garlic, lemon, and rosemary.
3. Tie your chicken with twine if needed. Pat the chicken dry.
4. Drizzle the olive oil all over and coat the entire chicken with a brush.
5. Shake the rub on the chicken and rub in until the chicken is covered.
6. Using the rotisserie shaft, push through the chicken and attach the rotisserie forks.
7. If desired, place aluminum foil onto the drip pan. (It makes for easier clean-up!)
8. Select Air Fry, Super Convection of the oven, set the temperature to 375ºF (190ºC). Set the time to 40 minutes. Check the temp in 5 minute increments after the 40 minutes. Select Start to begin preheating.
9. Once the unit has preheated, place the prepared chicken with the rotisserie shaft into the oven.
10. At 40 minutes, check the temperature every 5 minutes until the chicken reaches 165ºF (74ºC) in the breast, or 165ºF (85ºC) in the thigh.
11. Once cooking is complete, remove the chicken using the rotisserie handle and, using hot pads or gloves, carefully remove the chicken from the shaft.
12. Let the chicken sit, covered, for 5 to 10 minutes.
13. Slice and serve.

CHAPTER 11

DESSERTS

88	Oatmeal Raisin Bars
88	Lemony Apple Butter
89	Bourbon Bread Pudding
89	Baked Apples
90	Applesauce and Chocolate Brownies
90	Pineapple Galette
91	Ricotta Lemon Poppy Seed Cake
92	Spice Cookies
92	Chickpea Brownies
93	Chocolate Cake

Oatmeal Raisin Bars

Prep time: 15 minutes | Cook time: 15 minutes | Serves 8

- 1/3 cup all-purpose flour
- 1/4 teaspoon kosher salt
- 1/4 teaspoon baking powder
- 1/4 teaspoon ground cinnamon
- 1/4 cup light brown sugar, lightly packed
- 1/4 cup granulated sugar
- 1/2 cup canola oil
- 1 large egg
- 1 teaspoon vanilla extract
- 1 1/3 cups quick-cooking oats
- 1/3 cup raisins

1. Press Start/Cancel. Preheat the air fryer oven to 360°F (182°C).
2. In a large bowl, combine the all-purpose flour, kosher salt, baking powder, ground cinnamon, light brown sugar, granulated sugar, canola oil, egg, vanilla extract, quick-cooking oats, and raisins.
3. Spray a baking pan with nonstick cooking spray, then pour the oat mixture into the pan and press down to evenly distribute. Place the pan in the air fryer oven and insert at low position. Select Bake, Convection, and set time to 15 minutes, or until golden brown.
4. Remove from the air fryer oven and allow to cool in the pan on a wire rack for 20 minutes before slicing and serving.

Lemony Apple Butter

Prep time: 10 minutes | Cook time: 1 hour | Makes 1¼ cups

- Cooking spray
- 2 cups unsweetened applesauce
- 2/3 cup packed light brown sugar
- 3 tablespoons fresh lemon juice
- 1/2 teaspoon kosher salt
- 1/4 teaspoon ground cinnamon
- 1/8 teaspoon ground allspice

1. Press Start/Cancel. Preheat the air fryer oven to 340°F (171°C).
2. Spray a metal cake pan with cooking spray. Whisk together all the ingredients in a bowl until smooth, then pour into the greased pan. Set the pan in the air fryer oven and insert at low position. Select Bake, Convection, and set time to 1 hour until the apple mixture is caramelized, reduced to a thick purée, and fragrant.
3. Remove the pan from the air fryer oven, stir to combine the caramelized bits at the edge with the rest, then let cool completely to thicken.
4. Serve immediately.

Bourbon Bread Pudding

Prep time: 10 minutes | Cook time: 20 minutes | Serves 4

- 3 slices whole grain bread, cubed
- 1 large egg
- 1 cup whole milk
- 2 tablespoons bourbon
- ½ teaspoons vanilla extract
- ¼ cup maple syrup, divided
- ½ teaspoons ground cinnamon
- 2 teaspoons sparkling sugar

1. Press Start/Cancel. Preheat the air fryer oven to 270ºF (132ºC).
2. Spray a baking pan with nonstick cooking spray, then place the bread cubes in the pan.
3. In a medium bowl, whisk together the egg, milk, bourbon, vanilla extract, 3 tablespoons of maple syrup, and cinnamon. Pour the egg mixture over the bread and press down with a spatula to coat all the bread, then sprinkle the sparkling sugar on top.
4. Insert the pan at low position. Select Bake, Convection, and set time to 20 minutes.
5. Remove the pudding from the air fryer oven and allow to cool in the pan on a wire rack for 10 minutes. Drizzle the remaining 1 tablespoon of maple syrup on top. Slice and serve warm.

Baked Apples

Prep time: 5 minutes | Cook time: 10 minutes | Serves 4

- 4 small apples, cored and cut in half
- 2 tablespoons salted butter or coconut oil, melted
- 2 tablespoons sugar
- 1 teaspoon apple pie spice
- Ice cream, heavy cream, or whipped cream, for serving

1. Press Start/Cancel. Preheat the air fryer oven to 350ºF (177ºC).
2. Put the apples in a large bowl. Drizzle with the melted butter and sprinkle with the sugar and apple pie spice. Use the hands to toss, ensuring the apples are evenly coated.
3. Put the apples in the fry basket and insert at low position. Select Bake, Convection, and set time to 10 minutes. Pierce the apples with a fork to ensure they are tender.
4. Serve with ice cream, or top with a splash of heavy cream or a spoonful of whipped cream.

Applesauce and Chocolate Brownies

Prep time: 10 minutes | Cook time: 15 minutes | Serves 8

- ¼ cup unsweetened cocoa powder
- ¼ cup all-purpose flour
- ¼ teaspoon kosher salt
- ½ teaspoons baking powder
- 3 tablespoons unsalted butter, melted
- ½ cup granulated sugar
- 1 large egg
- 3 tablespoons unsweetened applesauce
- ¼ cup miniature semisweet chocolate chips
- Coarse sea salt, to taste

1. Press Start/Cancel. Preheat the air fryer oven to 300ºF (149ºC).
2. In a large bowl, whisk together the cocoa powder, all-purpose flour, kosher salt, and baking powder.
3. In a separate large bowl, combine the butter, granulated sugar, egg, and applesauce, then use a spatula to fold in the cocoa powder mixture and the chocolate chips until well combined.
4. Spray a baking pan with nonstick cooking spray, then pour the mixture into the pan. Place the pan in the air fryer oven and insert at low position. Select Bake, Convection, and set time to 15 minutes, or until a toothpick comes out clean when inserted in the middle.
5. Remove the brownies from the air fryer oven, sprinkle some coarse sea salt on top, and allow to cool in the pan on a wire rack for 20 minutes before cutting and serving.

Pineapple Galette

Prep time: 10 minutes | Cook time: 40 minutes | Serves 2

- ¼ medium-size pineapple, peeled, cored, and cut crosswise into ¼-inch-thick slices
- 2 tablespoons dark rum
- 1 teaspoon vanilla extract
- ½ teaspoon kosher salt
- Finely grated zest of ½ lime
- 1 store-bought sheet puff pastry, cut into an 8-inch round
- 3 tablespoons granulated sugar
- 2 tablespoons unsalted butter, cubed and chilled
- Coconut ice cream, for serving

1. Press Start/Cancel. Preheat the air fryer oven to 310ºF (154ºC).
2. In a small bowl, combine the pineapple slices, rum, vanilla, salt, and lime zest and let stand for at least 10 minutes to allow the pineapple to soak in the rum.

3. Meanwhile, press the puff pastry round into the bottom and up the sides of a round metal cake pan and use the tines of a fork to dock the bottom and sides.
4. Arrange the pineapple slices on the bottom of the pastry in more or less a single layer, then sprinkle with the sugar and dot with the butter. Drizzle with the leftover juices from the bowl. Put the pan in the air fryer oven and insert at low position. Select Bake, Convection, and set time to 40 minutes until the pastry is puffed and golden brown and the pineapple is lightly caramelized on top.
5. Transfer the pan to a wire rack to cool for 15 minutes. Unmold the galette from the pan and serve warm with coconut ice cream.

Ricotta Lemon Poppy Seed Cake

Prep time: 15 minutes | Cook time: 58 minutes | Serves 4

- Unsalted butter, at room temperature
- 1 cup almond flour
- ½ cup sugar
- 3 large eggs
- ¼ cup heavy cream
- ¼ cup full-fat ricotta cheese
- ¼ cup coconut oil, melted
- 2 tablespoons poppy seeds
- 1 teaspoon baking powder
- 1 teaspoon pure lemon extract
- Grated zest and juice of 1 lemon, plus more zest for garnish

1. Press Start/Cancel. Preheat the air fryer oven to 325ºF (163ºC).
2. Generously butter a round baking pan. Line the bottom of the pan with parchment paper cut to fit.
3. In a large bowl, combine the almond flour, sugar, eggs, cream, ricotta, coconut oil, poppy seeds, baking powder, lemon extract, lemon zest, and lemon juice. Beat with a hand mixer on medium speed until well blended and fluffy.
4. Pour the batter into the prepared pan. Cover the pan tightly with aluminum foil. Set the pan in the fry basket and insert at low position.
5. Select Bake, Convection, and set time to 45 minutes. Remove the foil and bake for 13 minutes more until a knife (do not use a toothpick) inserted into the center of the cake comes out clean.
6. Let the cake cool in the pan on a wire rack for 10 minutes. Remove the cake from pan and let it cool on the rack for 15 minutes before slicing.
7. Top with additional lemon zest, slice and serve.

Spice Cookies

Prep time: 15 minutes | Cook time: 12 minutes | Serves 4

- 4 tablespoons (½ stick) unsalted butter, at room temperature
- 2 tablespoons agave nectar
- 1 large egg
- 2 tablespoons water
- 2½ cups almond flour
- ½ cup sugar
- 2 teaspoons ground ginger
- 1 teaspoon ground cinnamon
- ½ teaspoon freshly grated nutmeg
- 1 teaspoon baking soda
- ¼ teaspoon kosher salt

1. Press Start/Cancel. Preheat the air fryer oven to 325ºF (163ºC).
2. Line the bottom of the fry basket with parchment paper cut to fit.
3. In a large bowl using a hand mixer, beat together the butter, agave, egg, and water on medium speed until fluffy.
4. Add the almond flour, sugar, ginger, cinnamon, nutmeg, baking soda, and salt. Beat on low speed until well combined.
5. Roll the dough into 2-tablespoon balls and arrange them on the parchment paper in the basket. Insert at low position. Select Bake, Convection, and set time to 12 minutes, or until the tops of cookies are lightly browned.
6. Transfer to a wire rack and let cool completely.
7. Serve immediately

Chickpea Brownies

Prep time: 10 minutes | Cook time: 20 minutes | Serves 6

- Vegetable oil
- 1 (15-ounce / 425-g) can chickpeas, drained and rinsed
- 4 large eggs
- ⅓ cup coconut oil, melted
- ⅓ cup honey
- 3 tablespoons unsweetened cocoa powder
- 1 tablespoon espresso powder (optional)
- 1 teaspoon baking powder
- 1 teaspoon baking soda
- ½ cup chocolate chips

1. Press Start/Cancel. Preheat the air fryer oven to 325ºF (163ºC).
2. Generously grease a baking pan with vegetable oil.
3. In a blender or food processor, combine the chickpeas, eggs, coconut oil, honey, cocoa powder, espresso powder (if using), baking powder, and baking soda. Blend or process until smooth. Transfer to the prepared pan and stir in the chocolate chips by hand.

4. Set the pan in the fry basket and insert at low position. Select Bake, Convection, and set time to 20 minutes, or until a toothpick inserted into the center comes out clean.
5. Let cool in the pan on a wire rack for 30 minutes before cutting into squares.
6. Serve immediately.

Chocolate Cake

Prep time: 10 minutes | Cook time: 55 minutes | Serves 4

- Unsalted butter, at room temperature
- 3 large eggs
- 1 cup almond flour
- ⅔ cup sugar
- ⅓ cup heavy cream
- ¼ cup coconut oil, melted
- ¼ cup unsweetened cocoa powder
- 1 teaspoon baking powder
- ¼ cup chopped walnuts

1. Press Start/Cancel. Preheat the air fryer oven to 400ºF (204ºC).
2. Generously butter a round baking pan. Line the bottom of the pan with parchment paper cut to fit.
3. In a large bowl, combine the eggs, almond flour, sugar, cream, coconut oil, cocoa powder, and baking powder. Beat with a hand mixer on medium speed until well blended and fluffy. (This will keep the cake from being too dense, as almond flour cakes can sometimes be.) Fold in the walnuts.
4. Pour the batter into the prepared pan. Cover the pan tightly with aluminum foil. Set the pan in the fry basket and insert at low position.
5. Select Bake, Convection, and set time to 45 minutes. Remove the foil and bake for 10 to 15 minutes more until a knife (do not use a toothpick) inserted into the center of the cake comes out clean.
6. Let the cake cool in the pan on a wire rack for 10 minutes. Remove the cake from the pan and let cool on the rack for 20 minutes before slicing and serving.

CHAPTER 12

HOLIDAY SPECIALS

96	Holiday Spicy Beef Roast
96	Lush Snack Mix
97	Mushroom and Green Bean Casserole
97	Eggnog Bread
98	Whole Chicken Roast
99	Hasselback Potatoes
99	Air Fried Spicy Olives
100	Bourbon Monkey Bread
101	Hearty Honey Yeast Rolls

Holiday Spicy Beef Roast

Prep time: 10 minutes | Cook time: 45 minutes | Serves 8

- 2 pounds (907 g) roast beef, at room temperature
- 2 tablespoons extra-virgin olive oil
- 1 teaspoon sea salt flakes
- 1 teaspoon black pepper, preferably freshly ground
- 1 teaspoon smoked paprika
- A few dashes of liquid smoke
- 2 jalapeño peppers, thinly sliced

1. Press Start/Cancel. Preheat the air fryer oven to 330ºF (166ºC).
2. Pat the roast dry using kitchen towels. Rub with extra-virgin olive oil and all seasonings along with liquid smoke. Transfer the roast to the food tray. Insert at low position.
3. Select Roast, Convection, and set time to 30 minutes. Turn the roast over and roast for additional 15 minutes.
4. Check for doneness using a meat thermometer and serve sprinkled with sliced jalapeños. Bon appétit!

Lush Snack Mix

Prep time: 10 minutes | Cook time: 11 minutes | Serves 10

- ½ cup honey
- 3 tablespoons butter, melted
- 1 teaspoon salt
- 2 cups sesame sticks
- 2 cup pumpkin seeds
- 2 cups granola
- 1 cup cashews
- 2 cups crispy corn puff cereal
- 2 cup mini pretzel crisps

1. In a bowl, combine the honey, butter, and salt.
2. In another bowl, mix the sesame sticks, pumpkin seeds, granola, cashews, corn puff cereal, and pretzel crisps.
3. Combine the contents of the two bowls.
4. Press Start/Cancel. Preheat the air fryer oven to 370ºF (188ºC).
5. Put the mixture in the fry basket and insert the fry basket at mid position. Select Air Fry, Convection, and set time to 11 minutes, shaking the basket frequently. Do this in two batches.
6. Put the snack mix on a cookie sheet and allow it to cool fully.
7. Serve immediately.

Mushroom and Green Bean Casserole

Prep time: 10 minutes | Cook time: 15 minutes | Serves 4

- 4 tablespoons unsalted butter
- ¼ cup diced yellow onion
- ½ cup chopped white mushrooms
- ½ cup heavy whipping cream
- 1 ounce (28 g) full-fat cream cheese
- ½ cup chicken broth
- ¼ teaspoon xanthan gum
- 1 pound (454 g) fresh green beans, edges trimmed
- ½ ounce (14 g) pork rinds, finely ground

1. In a medium skillet over medium heat, melt the butter. Sauté the onion and mushrooms until they become soft and fragrant, about 3 to 5 minutes.
2. Add the heavy whipping cream, cream cheese, and broth to the pan. Whisk until smooth. Bring to a boil and then reduce to a simmer. Sprinkle the xanthan gum into the pan and remove from heat.
3. Press Start/Cancel. Preheat the air fryer oven to 320ºF (160ºC).
4. Chop the green beans into 2-inch pieces and place into a baking dish. Pour the sauce mixture over them and stir until coated. Top the dish with ground pork rinds. Put into the fry basket and insert at low position. Select Bake, Convection, and set time to 15 minutes.
5. Top will be golden and green beans fork-tender when fully cooked. Serve warm.

Eggnog Bread

Prep time: 10 minutes | Cook time: 18 minutes | Serves 6 to 8

- 1 cup flour, plus more for dusting
- ¼ cup sugar
- 1 teaspoon baking powder
- ¼ teaspoon salt
- ¼ teaspoon nutmeg
- ½ cup eggnog
- 1 egg yolk
- 1 tablespoon plus 1 teaspoon butter, melted
- ¼ cup pecans
- ¼ cup chopped candied fruit (cherries, pineapple, or mixed fruits)
- Cooking spray

1. Press Start/Cancel. Preheat the air fryer oven to 360ºF (182ºC).
2. In a medium bowl, stir together the flour, sugar, baking powder, salt, and nutmeg.
3. Add eggnog, egg yolk, and butter. Mix well but do not beat.
4. Stir in nuts and fruit.

5. Spray a baking pan with cooking spray and dust with flour.
6. Spread batter into prepared pan and insert at low position. Select Bake, Convection, and set time to 18 minutes, or until top is dark golden brown and bread starts to pull away from sides of pan.
7. Serve immediately.

Whole Chicken Roast

Prep time: 10 minutes | Cook time: 1 hour | Serves 6

- 1 teaspoon salt
- 1 teaspoon Italian seasoning
- ½ teaspoon freshly ground black pepper
- ½ teaspoon paprika
- ½ teaspoon garlic powder
- ½ teaspoon onion powder
- 2 tablespoons olive oil, plus more as needed
- 1 (4-pound / 1.8-kg) fryer chicken

1. Press Start/Cancel. Preheat the air fryer oven to 360ºF (182ºC).
2. Grease the fry basket lightly with olive oil.
3. In a small bowl, mix the salt, Italian seasoning, pepper, paprika, garlic powder, and onion powder.
4. Remove any giblets from the chicken. Pat the chicken dry thoroughly with paper towels, including the cavity.
5. Brush the chicken all over with the olive oil and rub it with the seasoning mixture.
6. Truss the chicken or tie the legs with butcher's twine. This will make it easier to flip the chicken during cooking.
7. Put the chicken in the fry basket, breast-side down. Insert the fry basket at mid position.
8. Select Air Fry, Convection, and set time to 30 minutes. Flip the chicken over and baste it with any drippings collected in the bottom drawer of the air fryer oven. Lightly brush the chicken with olive oil.
9. Air fry for 20 minutes. Flip the chicken over one last time and air fry until a thermometer inserted into the thickest part of the thigh reaches at least 165ºF (74ºC) and it's crispy and golden, 10 more minutes. Continue to cook, checking every 5 minutes until the chicken reaches the correct internal temperature.
10. Let the chicken rest for 10 minutes before carving and serving.

Hasselback Potatoes

Prep time: 5 minutes | Cook time: 45 minutes | Serves 4

- 4 russet potatoes, peeled
- Salt and freshly ground black pepper, to taste
- ¼ cup grated Parmesan cheese
- Cooking spray

1. Press Start/Cancel. Preheat the air fryer oven to 400ºF (204ºC).
2. Spray the fry basket lightly with cooking spray.
3. Make thin parallel cuts into each potato, ⅛-inch to ¼-inch apart, stopping at about ½ of the way through. The potato needs to stay intact along the bottom.
4. Spray the potatoes with cooking spray and use the hands or a silicone brush to completely coat the potatoes lightly in oil.
5. Put the potatoes, sliced side up, in the fry basket in a single layer. Leave a little room between each potato. Sprinkle the potatoes lightly with salt and black pepper.
6. Insert the fry basket at mid position. Select Air Fry, Convection, and set time to 20 minutes. Reposition the potatoes and spritz lightly with cooking spray again. Air fry until the potatoes are fork-tender and crispy and browned, another 25 minutes.
7. Sprinkle the potatoes with Parmesan cheese and serve.

Air Fried Spicy Olives

Prep time: 10 minutes | Cook time: 5 minutes | Serves 4

- 12 ounces (340 g) pitted black extra-large olives
- ¼ cup all-purpose flour
- 1 cup panko bread crumbs
- 2 teaspoons dried thyme
- 1 teaspoon red pepper flakes
- 1 teaspoon smoked paprika
- 1 egg beaten with 1 tablespoon water
- Vegetable oil for spraying

1. Press Start/Cancel. Preheat the air fryer oven to 400ºF (204ºC).
2. Drain the olives and place them on a paper towel–lined plate to dry.
3. Put the flour on a plate. Combine the panko, thyme, red pepper flakes, and paprika on a separate plate. Dip an olive in the flour, shaking off any excess, then coat with egg mixture. Dredge the olive in the panko mixture, pressing to make the crumbs adhere, and place the breaded olive on a platter. Repeat with the remaining olives.

4. Spray the olives with oil and place them in a single layer in the fry basket. Work in batches if necessary so as not to overcrowd the basket.
5. Insert the fry basket at mid position. Select Air Fry, Convection, and set time to 5 minutes, or until the breading is browned and crispy.
6. Serve warm

Bourbon Monkey Bread

Prep time: 15 minutes | Cook time: 25 minutes | Serves 6 to 8

- 1 (16.3-ounce / 462-g) can store-bought refrigerated biscuit dough
- ¼ cup packed light brown sugar
- 1 teaspoon ground cinnamon
- ½ teaspoon freshly grated nutmeg
- ½ teaspoon ground ginger
- ½ teaspoon kosher salt
- ¼ teaspoon ground allspice
- ⅛ teaspoon ground cloves
- 4 tablespoons (½ stick) unsalted butter, melted
- ½ cup powdered sugar
- 2 teaspoons bourbon
- 2 tablespoons chopped candied cherries
- 2 tablespoons chopped pecans

1. Press Start/Cancel. Preheat the air fryer oven to 310ºF (154ºC).
2. Open the can and separate the biscuits, then cut each into quarters. Toss the biscuit quarters in a large bowl with the brown sugar, cinnamon, nutmeg, ginger, salt, allspice, and cloves until evenly coated. Transfer the dough pieces and any sugar left in the bowl to a round cake pan, metal cake pan, or foil pan and drizzle evenly with the melted butter. Put the pan in the air fryer oven and insert at low position.
3. Select Bake, Convection, and set time to 25 minutes, or until the monkey bread is golden brown and cooked through in the middle. Transfer the pan to a wire rack and let cool completely. Unmold from the pan.
4. In a small bowl, whisk the powdered sugar and the bourbon into a smooth glaze. Drizzle the glaze over the cooled monkey bread and, while the glaze is still wet, sprinkle with the cherries and pecans to serve.

Hearty Honey Yeast Rolls

Prep time: 10 minutes | Cook time: 20 minutes | Makes 8 rolls

- ¼ cup whole milk, heated to 115°F (46°C) in the microwave
- ½ teaspoon active dry yeast
- 1 tablespoon honey
- ⅔ cup all-purpose flour, plus more for dusting
- ½ teaspoon kosher salt
- 2 tablespoons unsalted butter, at room temperature, plus more for greasing
- Flaky sea salt, to taste

1. In a large bowl, whisk together the milk, yeast, and honey and let stand until foamy, about 10 minutes.
2. Stir in the flour and salt until just combined. Stir in the butter until absorbed. Scrape the dough onto a lightly floured work surface and knead until smooth, about 6 minutes. Transfer the dough to a lightly greased bowl, cover loosely with a sheet of plastic wrap or a kitchen towel, and let sit until nearly doubled in size, about 1 hour.
3. Uncover the dough, lightly press it down to expel the bubbles, then portion it into 8 equal pieces. Prep the work surface by wiping it clean with a damp paper towel (if there is flour on the work surface, it will prevent the dough from sticking lightly to the surface, which helps it form a ball). Roll each piece into a ball by cupping the palm of the hand around the dough against the work surface and moving the heel of the hand in a circular motion while using the thumb to contain the dough and tighten it into a perfectly round ball. Once all the balls are formed, nestle them side by side in the fry basket.
4. Cover the rolls loosely with a kitchen towel or a sheet of plastic wrap and let sit until lightly risen and puffed, 20 to 30 minutes.
5. Press Start/Cancel. Preheat the air fryer oven to 270°F (132°C).
6. Uncover the rolls and gently brush with more butter, being careful not to press the rolls too hard. Transfer to the fry basket. Insert the fry basket at mid position. Select Air Fry, Convection, and set time to 12 minutes, or until the rolls are light golden brown and fluffy.
7. Remove the rolls from the air fryer oven and brush liberally with more butter, if you like, and sprinkle each roll with a pinch of sea salt. Serve warm.

CHAPTER 13

SAUCES, DIPS, AND DRESSINGS

- 104 Red Buffalo Sauce
- 104 Cauliflower Alfredo Sauce
- 105 Balsamic Dressing
- 105 Avocado Dressing
- 105 Ginger Sweet Sauce
- 106 Pico de Gallo
- 106 Hemp Dressing
- 106 Cashew Mayo

Sauces, Dips, and Dressings | 103

Red Buffalo Sauce

Prep time: 5 minutes | Cook time: 20 minutes | Makes 2 cups

- ¼ cup olive oil
- 4 garlic cloves, roughly chopped
- 1 (5-ounce / 142-g) small red onion, roughly chopped
- 6 red chiles, roughly chopped (about 2 ounces / 56 g in total)
- 1 cup water
- ½ cup apple cider vinegar
- ½ teaspoon salt
- ½ teaspoon freshly ground black pepper

1. In a large nonstick sauté pan, heat ¼ cup olive oil over medium-high heat. Once it's hot, add the garlic, onion, and chiles. Cook for 5 minutes, stirring occasionally, until onions are golden brown.
2. Add the water and bring to a boil. Cook for about 10 minutes or until the water has nearly evaporated.
3. Transfer the cooked onion and chile mixture to a food processor or blender and blend briefly to combine. Add the apple cider vinegar, salt, and pepper. Blend again for 30 seconds.
4. Using a mesh sieve, strain the sauce into a bowl. Use a spoon or spatula to scrape and press all the liquid from the pulp.

Cauliflower Alfredo Sauce

Prep time: 2 minutes | Cook time: 0 minutes | Makes 4 cups

- 2 tablespoons olive oil
- 6 garlic cloves, minced
- 3 cups unsweetened almond milk
- 1 (1-pound / 454-g) head cauliflower, cut into florets
- 1 teaspoon salt
- ¼ teaspoon freshly ground black pepper
- Juice of 1 lemon
- 4 tablespoons nutritional yeast

1. In a medium saucepan, heat the olive oil over medium-high heat. Add the garlic and sauté for 1 minute or until fragrant. Add the almond milk, stir, and bring to a boil.
2. Gently add the cauliflower. Stir in the salt and pepper and return to a boil. Continue cooking over medium-high heat for 5 minutes or until the cauliflower is soft. Stir frequently and reduce heat if needed to prevent the liquid from boiling over.
3. Carefully transfer the cauliflower and cooking liquid to a food processor, using a slotted spoon to scoop out the larger pieces of cauliflower before pouring in the liquid. Add the lemon and nutritional yeast and blend for 1 to 2 minutes until smooth.
4. Serve immediately.

Balsamic Dressing

Prep time: 5 minutes | Cook time: 0 minutes | Makes 1 cup

- 2 tablespoons Dijon mustard
- ¼ cup balsamic vinegar
- ¾ cup olive oil

1. Put all ingredients in a jar with a tight-fitting lid. Put on the lid and shake vigorously until thoroughly combined. Refrigerate until ready to use and shake well before serving.

Avocado Dressing

Prep time: 5 minutes | Cook time: 0 minutes | Makes 12 tablespoons

- 1 large avocado, pitted and peeled
- ½ cup water
- 2 tablespoons tahini
- 2 tablespoons freshly squeezed lemon juice
- 1 teaspoon dried basil
- 1 teaspoon white wine vinegar
- 1 garlic clove
- ¼ teaspoon pink Himalayan salt
- ¼ teaspoon freshly ground black pepper

1. Combine all the ingredients in a food processor and blend until smooth.

Ginger Sweet Sauce

Prep time: 5 minutes | Cook time: 5 minutes | Makes ⅔ cup

- 3 tablespoons ketchup
- 2 tablespoons water
- 2 tablespoons maple syrup
- 1 tablespoon rice vinegar
- 2 teaspoons peeled minced fresh ginger root
- 2 teaspoons soy sauce (or tamari, which is a gluten-free option)
- 1 teaspoon cornstarch

1. In a small saucepan over medium heat, combine all the ingredients and stir continuously for 5 minutes, or until slightly thickened. Enjoy warm or cold.

Pico de Gallo

Prep time: 5 minutes | Cook time: 0 minutes | Serves 2

- 3 large tomatoes, chopped
- ½ small red onion, diced
- ⅛ cup chopped fresh cilantro
- 3 garlic cloves, chopped
- 2 tablespoons chopped pickled jalapeño pepper
- 1 tablespoon lime juice
- ¼ teaspoon pink Himalayan salt (optional)

1. In a medium bowl, combine all the ingredients and mix with a wooden spoon.

Hemp Dressing

Prep time: 5 minutes | Cook time: 0 minutes | Makes 12 tablespoons

- ½ cup white wine vinegar
- ¼ cup tahini
- ¼ cup water
- 1 tablespoon hemp seeds
- ½ tablespoon freshly squeezed lemon juice
- 1 teaspoon garlic powder
- 1 teaspoon dried oregano
- 1 teaspoon dried basil
- 1 teaspoon red pepper flakes
- ½ teaspoon onion powder
- ½ teaspoon pink Himalayan salt
- ½ teaspoon freshly ground black pepper

1. In a bowl, combine all the ingredients and whisk until mixed well.

Cashew Mayo

Prep time: 5 minutes | Cook time: 0 minutes | Makes 18 tablespoons

1 cup cashews, soaked in hot water for at least 1 hour
¼ cup plus 3 tablespoons milk
1 tablespoon apple cider vinegar
1 tablespoon freshly squeezed lemon juice
1 tablespoon Dijon mustard
1 tablespoon aquafaba
⅛ teaspoon pink Himalayan salt

1. In a food processor, combine all the ingredients and blend until creamy and smooth.

Appendix 1 Measurement Conversion Chart

VOLUME EQUIVALENTS(DRY)

US STANDARD	METRIC (APPROXIMATE)
1/8 teaspoon	0.5 mL
1/4 teaspoon	1 mL
1/2 teaspoon	2 mL
3/4 teaspoon	4 mL
1 teaspoon	5 mL
1 tablespoon	15 mL
1/4 cup	59 mL
1/2 cup	118 mL
3/4 cup	177 mL
1 cup	235 mL
2 cups	475 mL
3 cups	700 mL
4 cups	1 L

WEIGHT EQUIVALENTS

US STANDARD	METRIC (APPROXIMATE)
1 ounce	28 g
2 ounces	57 g
5 ounces	142 g
10 ounces	284 g
15 ounces	425 g
16 ounces (1 pound)	455 g
1.5 pounds	680 g
2 pounds	907 g

VOLUME EQUIVALENTS(LIQUID)

US STANDARD	US STANDARD (OUNCES)	METRIC (APPROXIMATE)
2 tablespoons	1 fl.oz.	30 mL
1/4 cup	2 fl.oz.	60 mL
1/2 cup	4 fl.oz.	120 mL
1 cup	8 fl.oz.	240 mL
1 1/2 cup	12 fl.oz.	355 mL
2 cups or 1 pint	16 fl.oz.	475 mL
4 cups or 1 quart	32 fl.oz.	1 L
1 gallon	128 fl.oz.	4 L

TEMPERATURES EQUIVALENTS

FAHRENHEIT(F)	CELSIUS(C) (APPROXIMATE)
225 °F	107 °C
250 °F	120 °C
275 °F	135 °C
300 °F	150 °C
325 °F	160 °C
350 °F	180 °C
375 °F	190 °C
400 °F	205 °C
425 °F	220 °C
450 °F	235 °C
475 °F	245 °C
500 °F	260 °C

Appendix 2 Air Fryer Cooking Chart

Beef

Item	Temp (°F)	Time (mins)	Item	Temp (°F)	Time (mins)
Beef Eye Round Roast (4 lbs.)	400 °F	45 to 55	Meatballs (1-inch)	370 °F	7
Burger Patty (4 oz.)	370 °F	16 to 20	Meatballs (3-inch)	380 °F	10
Filet Mignon (8 oz.)	400 °F	18	Ribeye, bone-in (1-inch, 8 oz)	400 °F	10 to 15
Flank Steak (1.5 lbs.)	400 °F	12	Sirloin steaks (1-inch, 12 oz)	400 °F	9 to 14
Flank Steak (2 lbs.)	400 °F	20 to 28			

Chicken

Item	Temp (°F)	Time (mins)	Item	Temp (°F)	Time (mins)
Breasts, bone in (1 ¼ lb.)	370 °F	25	Legs, bone-in (1 ¾ lb.)	380 °F	30
Breasts, boneless (4 oz)	380 °F	12	Thighs, boneless (1 ½ lb.)	380 °F	18 to 20
Drumsticks (2 ½ lb.)	370 °F	20	Wings (2 lb.)	400 °F	12
Game Hen (halved 2 lb.)	390 °F	20	Whole Chicken	360 °F	75
Thighs, bone-in (2 lb.)	380 °F	22	Tenders	360 °F	8 to 10

Pork & Lamb

Item	Temp (°F)	Time (mins)	Item	Temp (°F)	Time (mins)
Bacon (regular)	400 °F	5 to 7	Pork Tenderloin	370 °F	15
Bacon (thick cut)	400 °F	6 to 10	Sausages	380 °F	15
Pork Loin (2 lb.)	360 °F	55	Lamb Loin Chops (1-inch thick)	400 °F	8 to 12
Pork Chops, bone in (1-inch, 6.5 oz)	400 °F	12	Rack of Lamb (1.5 – 2 lb.)	380 °F	22

Fish & Seafood

Item	Temp (°F)	Time (mins)	Item	Temp (°F)	Time (mins)
Calamari (8 oz)	400 °F	4	Tuna Steak	400 °F	7 to 10
Fish Fillet (1-inch, 8 oz)	400 °F	10	Scallops	400 °F	5 to 7
Salmon, fillet (6 oz)	380 °F	12	Shrimp	400 °F	5
Swordfish steak	400 °F	10			

Vegetables

INGREDIENT	AMOUNT	PREPARATION	OIL	TEMP	COOK TIME
Asparagus	2 bunches	Cut in half, trim stems	2 Tbsp	420°F	12-15 mins
Beets	1½ lbs	Peel, cut in ½-inch cubes	1Tbsp	390°F	28-30 mins
Bell peppers (for roasting)	4 peppers	Cut in quarters, remove seeds	1Tbsp	400°F	15-20 mins
Broccoli	1 large head	Cut in 1-2-inch florets	1Tbsp	400°F	15-20 mins
Brussels sprouts	1lb	Cut in half, remove stems	1Tbsp	425°F	15-20 mins
Carrots	1lb	Peel, cut in ¼-inch rounds	1 Tbsp	425°F	10-15 mins
Cauliflower	1 head	Cut in 1-2-inch florets	2 Tbsp	400°F	20-22 mins
Corn on the cob	7 ears	Whole ears, remove husks	1 Tbps	400°F	14-17 mins
Green beans	1 bag (12 oz)	Trim	1 Tbps	420°F	18-20 mins
Kale (for chips)	4 oz	Tear into pieces, remove stems	None	325°F	5-8 mins
Mushrooms	16 oz	Rinse, slice thinly	1 Tbps	390°F	25-30 mins
Potatoes, russet	1½ lbs	Cut in 1-inch wedges	1 Tbps	390°F	25-30 mins
Potatoes, russet	1lb	Hand-cut fries, soak 30 mins in cold water, then pat dry	½ -3 Tbps	400°F	25-28 mins
Potatoes, sweet	1lb	Hand-cut fries, soak 30 mins in cold water, then pat dry	1 Tbps	400°F	25-28 mins
Zucchini	1lb	Cut in eighths lengthwise, then cut in half	1 Tbps	400°F	15-20 mins

Appendix 3 Recipe Index

A
Air Fried Beef Roast   79
Air Fried Broccoli   12
Air Fried Spicy Olives   99
Almond-Crusted Chicken Nuggets   52
Apple and Carrot Stuffed Rotisserie Turkey   80
Applesauce and Chocolate Brownies   90
Apricot Glazed Turkey Tenderloin   51
Avocado Dressing   105

B
Bacon and Pear Stuffed Pork Chops   63
Bacon-Wrapped Beef Hot Dog   14
Baked Apples   89
Baked Chorizo Scotch Eggs   16
Baked Ricotta   22
Balsamic Dressing   105
BBQ Pork Steaks   60
Beef and Mango Skewers   23
Beef and Pork Sausage Meatloaf   58
Beef and Spinach Rolls   58
Beef Chuck Cheeseburgers   59
Beef Chuck with Brussels Sprouts   61
Bistro Potato Wedges   13
Bourbon Bread Pudding   89
Bourbon Monkey Bread   100
Bourbon Rotisserie Pork Shoulder   83
Breakfast Sausage and Cauliflower   30

C
Carrot and Celery Croquettes   14
Cashew Mayo   106
Cashew Stuffed Mushrooms   37
Cauliflower Alfredo Sauce   104
Cheesy Chicken Sandwich   43
Cheesy Greens Sandwich   44
Cheesy Potato Patties   15
Cheesy Sausage Balls   13
Chicken Pita Sandwich   42
Chicken with Pineapple and Peach   53
Chicken-Lettuce Wraps   46
Chickpea Brownies   92
Chocolate Cake   93
Classic British Breakfast   27
Classic Sloppy Joes   44
Coconut-Crusted Shrimp   20
Cornmeal-Crusted Trout Fingers   70
Crab Cakes with Sriracha Mayonnaise   68
Cranberry Curry Chicken   49
Crispy Coconut Shrimp   67
Crispy Jicama Fries   37
Crispy Spiced Chickpeas   19
Crunchy Air Fried Cod Fillets   75
Curried Orange Honey Chicken   53

E
Easy Roasted Asparagus   16
Easy Rosemary Green Beans   38
Egg and Bacon Muffins   31
Eggnog Bread   97

G
Ginger Sweet Sauce   105
Golden Avocado Tempura   31
Greek Lamb Rack   57
Greek Rotisserie Lamb Leg   84

H-I
Hasselback Potatoes   99
Hearty Honey Yeast Rolls   101
Hemp Dressing   106
Holiday Spicy Beef Roast   96
Honey Glazed Rotisserie Ham   78
Italian Lamb Chops with Avocado Mayo   57

J-K
Jerk Chicken Leg Quarters 50
Kale and Beef Omelet 59

L
Lemon Chicken and Spinach Salad 49
Lemon Garlic Chicken 52
Lemony Apple Butter 88
Lemony Chicken Drumsticks 23
Lush Snack Mix 96
Lush Vegetables Roast 34

M-N
Marinated Medium Rare Rotisserie Beef 81
Moroccan Spiced Halibut with Chickpea Salad 73
Mushroom and Green Bean Casserole 97
Nugget and Veggie Taco Wraps 43

O
Oatmeal Raisin Bars 88
Onion Omelet 28
Orange-Mustard Glazed Salmon 69

P
Parmesan Ranch Risotto 28
Parmesan Sausage Egg Muffins 30
Pecan-Crusted Turkey Cutlets 54
Pico de Gallo 106
Pineapple Galette 90
Pork Medallions with Radicchio and Endive Salad 60
Potato and Broccoli with Tofu Scramble 34
Potatoes Lyonnaise 29

R
Ratatouille 35
Red Buffalo Sauce 104
Red Wine Rotisserie Lamb Leg 82
Ricotta Lemon Poppy Seed Cake 91

Roasted Cod with Lemon-Garlic Potatoes 72
Roasted Eggplant Slices 35
Roasted Potatoes and Asparagus 38
Roasted Salmon Fillets 67
Rosemary-Garlic Shoestring Fries 22
Rotisserie Chicken with Lemon 78

S
Shishito Peppers with Herb Dressing 24
Simple Pea Delight 15
Smoky Chicken Sandwich 45
Sole and Asparagus Bundles 71
Spice Cookies 92
Spiced Mixed Nuts 19
Spiced Sweet Potato Fries 21
Spicy Chicken Wings 20
Spinach and Beef Braciole 64
Sriracha Honey Pork Tenderloin 80
Sun-dried Tomato Crusted Chops 62
Super Easy Bacon Cups 27
Super Vegetable Burger 36
Sweet Corn and Carrot Fritters 12
Swordfish Skewers with Caponata 74

T-V
Tex-Mex Chicken Breasts 50
Thai Shrimp Skewers with Peanut Dipping Sauce 69
Tomato and Mozzarella Bruschetta 29
Tuna and Lettuce Wraps 42
Tuna Muffin Sandwich 41
Turkey and Cranberry Quesadillas 51
Veggie Salsa Wraps 41

W
Whole Chicken Roast 98
Whole Rotisserie Chicken 85

Z
Zucchini Balls 36

Milton Keynes UK
Ingram Content Group UK Ltd.
UKHW030633150224
437794UK00002B/49